WHAT IS CALLED THINKING?

RELIGIOUS PERSPECTIVES • VOLUME TWENTY-ONE

WHAT IS CALLED THINKING?

by MARTIN HEIDEGGER

A Translation of *Was Heisst Denken?*
by
Fred D. Wieck and J. Glenn Gray

With an Introduction by J. Glenn Gray

1817

HARPER & ROW, PUBLISHERS

NEW YORK, EVANSTON, AND LONDON

Originally published by Max Niemeyer Verlag, Tuebingen under the title *Was Heisst Denken?*, copyright 1954 by Max Niemeyer Verlag, Tuebingen. English translation by Fred D. Wieck and J. Glenn Gray.

FIRST EDITION

LIBRARY OF CONGRESS CATALOG CARD NUMBER: 68–17591

E-S

MARTIN HEIDEGGER
WORKS

General Editor J. Glenn Gray
Colorado College

———

Also by Martin Heidegger

BEING AND TIME
DISCOURSE ON THINKING
(*Gelassenheit*)

RELIGIOUS PERSPECTIVES

VOLUMES ALREADY PUBLISHED

CONTENTS

CONTENTS

RELIGIOUS PERSPECTIVES
Its Meaning and Purpose

RELIGIOUS PERSPECTIVES represents a quest for the rediscovery of man. It constitutes an effort to define man's search for the essence of being in order that he may have a knowledge of goals. It is an endeavor to show that there is no possibility of achieving an understanding of man's total nature on the basis of phenomena known by the analytical method alone. It hopes to point to the false antinomy between revelation and reason, faith and knowledge, grace and nature, courage and anxiety. Mathematics, physics, philosophy, biology, and religion, in spite of their almost complete independence, have begun to sense their interrelatedness and to become aware of that mode of cognition which teaches that "the light is not without but within me, and I myself am the light."

Modern man is threatened by a world created by himself. He is faced with the conversion of mind to naturalism, a dogmatic secularism and an opposition to a belief in the transcendent. He begins to see, however, that the universe is given not as one existing and one perceived but as the unity of subject and object; that the barrier between them cannot be said to have been dissolved as the result of recent experience in the physical sciences, since this barrier has never existed. Confronted with the question of meaning, he is summoned to rediscover and scrutinize the immutable and the permanent which constitute the dynamic, unifying aspect of life as well as the principle of differentiation; to reconcile identity and diversity, immutability and unrest. He begins to recognize that just as every person descends by his particular path, so he is able to ascend, and this ascent aims at

xi

a return to the source of creation, an inward home from which he has become estranged.

It is the hope of RELIGIOUS PERSPECTIVES that the rediscovery of man will point the way to the rediscovery of God. To this end a rediscovery of first principles should constitute part of the quest. These principles, not to be superseded by new discoveries, are not those of historical worlds that come to be and perish. They are to be sought in the heart and spirit of man, and no interpretation of a merely historical or scientific universe can guide the search. RELIGIOUS PERSPECTIVES attempts not only to ask dispassionately what the nature of God is, but also to restore to human life at least the hypothesis of God and the symbols that relate to him. It endeavors to show that man is faced with the metaphysical question of the truth of religion while he encounters the empirical question of its effects on the life of humanity and its meaning for society. Religion is here distinguished from theology and its doctrinal forms and is intended to denote the feelings, aspirations, and acts of men, as they relate to total reality. For we are all in search of reality, of a reality which is there whether we know it or not; and the search is of our own making but reality is not.

RELIGIOUS PERSPECTIVES is nourished by the spiritual and intellectual energy of world thought, by those religious and ethical leaders who are not merely spectators but scholars deeply involved in the critical problems common to all religions. These thinkers recognize that human morality and human ideals thrive only when set in a context of a transcendent attitude toward religion and that by pointing to the ground of identity and the common nature of being in the religious experience of man, the essential nature of religion may be defined. Thus, they are committed to reevaluate the meaning of everlastingness, an experience which has been lost and which is the content of that *visio Dei* constituting the structure of all religions. It is the many absorbed everlastingly into the ultimate unity, a unity subsuming what Whitehead calls the fluency of God and the everlastingness of passing experience.

These volumes seek to show that the unity of which we speak consists in a certitude emanating from the nature of man who seeks God and the nature of God who seeks man. Such certitude

bathes in an intuitive act of cognition, participating in the divine
essence and is related to the natural spirituality of intelligence.
This is not by any means to say that there is an equivalence of all
faiths in the traditional religions of human history. It is, however,
to emphasize the distinction between the spiritual and the temporal which all religions acknowledge. For duration of thought
is composed of instants superior to time, and is an intuition of
the permanence of existence and its metahistorical reality. In
fact, the symbol[1] itself found on cover and jacket of each volume
of RELIGIOUS PERSPECTIVES is the visible sign or representation of
the essence, immediacy, and timelessness of religious experience;
the one immutable center, which may be analogically related to
being in pure act, moving with centrifugal and ecumenical necessity outward into the manifold modes, yet simultaneously, with
dynamic centripetal power and with full intentional energy, returning to the source. Through the very diversity of its authors,
the Series shows that the basic and poignant concern of every
faith is to point to, and overcome the crisis in our apocalyptic
epoch—the crisis of man's separation from man and of man's
separation from God—the failure of love. The authors endeavor,
moreover, to illustrate the truth that the human heart is able, and
even yearns, to go to the very lengths of God; that the darkness
and cold, the frozen spiritual misery of recent times are breaking,
cracking, and beginning to move, yielding to efforts to overcome
spiritual muteness and moral paralysis. In this way, it is hoped,
the immediacy of pain and sorrow, the primacy of tragedy and
suffering in human life, may be transmuted into a spiritual and
moral triumph. For the uniqueness of man lies in his capacity for
self-transcendence.

RELIGIOUS PERSPECTIVES is therefore an effort to explore the
meaning of God, an exploration which constitutes an aspect of
man's intrinsic nature, part of his ontological substance. This
Series grows out of an abiding concern that in spite of the release
of man's creative energy which science has in part accomplished,
this very science has overturned the essential order of nature.
Shrewd as man's calculations have become concerning his means,
his choice of ends which was formerly correlated with belief in

[1] From the original design by Leo Katz.

God, with absolute criteria of conduct, has become witless. God is not to be treated as an exception to metaphysical principles, invoked to prevent their collapse. He is rather their chief exemplification, the sources of all potentiality. The personal reality of freedom and providence, of will and conscience, may demonstrate that "he who knows" commands a depth of consciousness inaccessible to the profane man, and is capable of that transfiguration which prevents the twisting of all good to ignominy. This religious content of experience is not within the province of science to bestow; it corrects the error of treating the scientific account as if it were itself metaphysical or religious; it challenges the tendency to make a religion of science—or a science of religion—a dogmatic act which destroys the moral dynamic of man. Indeed, many men of science are confronted with unexpected implications of their own thought and are beginning to accept, for instance, the trans-spatial and trans-temporal dimension in the nature of reality.

RELIGIOUS PERSPECTIVES attempts to show the fallacy of the apparent irrelevance of God in history. This series submits that no convincing image of man can arise, in spite of the many ways in which human thought has tried to reach it, without a philosophy of human nature and human freedom which does not exclude God. This image of *Homo cum Deo* implies the highest conceivable freedom, the freedom to step into the very fabric of the universe, a new formula for man's collaboration with the creative process and the only one which is able to protect man from the terror of existence. This image implies further that the mind and conscience are capable of making genuine discriminations and thereby may reconcile the serious tensions between the secular and religious, the profane and sacred. The idea of the sacred lies in what it *is*, timeless existence. By emphasizing timeless existence against reason as a reality, we are liberated, in our communion with the eternal, from the otherwise unbreakable rule of "before and after." Then we are able to admit that all forms, all symbols in religions, by their negation of error and their affirmation of the actuality of truth, make it possible to experience that *knowing* which is above knowledge, and that dynamic passage of the universe to unending unity.

God is here interpreted not as a heteronomous being issuing

commandments but as the *Tatt-Twam-Asi:* "Do unto others as you would have others do unto you. For I am the Lord." This does not mean a commandment from on high but rather a self-realization through "the other"; since the isolated individual is unthinkable and meaningless. Man becomes man by recognizing his true nature as a creature capable of will and decision. For then the divine and the sacred become manifest. And though he believes in choices, he is no Utopian expecting the "coming of the kingdom." Man, individually and collectively, is losing the chains which have bound him to the inexorable demands of nature. The constraints are diminishing and an infinity of choices becomes available to him. Thus man himself, from the sources of his ontological being, at last must decide what is the *bonum et malum.* And though the anonymous forces which in the past have set the constraints do indeed threaten him with total anarchy and with perhaps a worse tyranny than he experienced in past history, he nevertheless begins to see that preceding the moral issue is the cognitive problem: the perception of those conditions for life which permit mankind to fulfill itself and to accept the truth that beyond scientific, discursive knowledge is nondiscursive, intuitive awareness. And, I suggest, this is not to secularize God but rather to gather him into the heart of the nature of matter and indeed of life itself.

The volumes in this Series seek to challenge the crisis which separates, to make reasonable a religion that binds, and to present the numinous reality within the experience of man. Insofar as the Series succeeds in this quest, it will direct mankind toward a reality that is eternal and away from a preoccupation with that which is illusory and ephemeral.

For man is now confronted with his burden and his greatness: "He calleth to me, Watchman, what of the night? Watchman, what of the night?"[2] Perhaps the anguish in the human soul may be assuaged by the answer, by the *assimilation* of the person in God: "The morning cometh, and also the night: if ye will inquire, inquire ye: return, come."[3]

RUTH NANDA ANSHEN

2 Isaiah 21:11.
3 Isaiah 21:12.

INTRODUCTION

by J. Glenn Gray

What Is Called Thinking? is a course of university lectures.
Martin Heidegger delivered these lectures to his students
during the winter and summer semesters of 1951 and 1952
at the University of Freiburg. They were the last before his
formal retirement from the university. They were also the
first lectures he was permitted to give there since 1944,
when he was drafted by the Nazis into the people's militia
(*Volkssturm*) and was afterwards forbidden to teach by
the French occupying powers.

What this long interruption in his teaching activity must
have cost him is not difficult to guess, for Heidegger is above
all else a teacher. It is no accident that nearly all his publications since *Being and Time* (1927) were first lectures or
seminar discussions. For him the spoken word is greatly
superior to the written, as it was for Plato. In this book he
names Socrates, a teacher not an author, "the purest thinker
of the West."

As his succinct remarks about teaching early in these
lectures bear witness, Heidegger regards teaching as an
exalted activity which has nothing to do with "becoming a
famous professor" or an expert in one's field. Instead, he
likens it to the master-apprentice relation of the medieval
guilds, where the purpose of the teaching craft is to "let
learning occur." This can take place only when the teacher

is "more teachable than the apprentices," able to impart by his own example the proper relatedness to the subject matter being learned. In the present lectures it is evident that Heidegger is first and foremost preoccupied with the students before him, only secondarily with the wider circle of readers who will necessarily miss the vital character and nuances of the spoken word.

In order to aid these students in maintaining continuity in lectures delivered at weekly intervals, Heidegger provided in every case a summary of the preceding lecture, a summary which is also a transition to the new material. At his expressed wish we have placed these *Stundenübergänge* at the beginning of each lecture, rather than grouping them at the back of the two parts of the book as in the German edition. Though Heidegger rarely summarizes exactly what he said the previous week, this procedure does make for considerable repetition. Such repetition occurs naturally in every lecture course and these lectures were *not* revised for publication, as a note on the flyleaf informs us. But for a man who puts as much emphasis as Heidegger on the *way* anything is said and who reflects on what he himself thought a week earlier, the repetition of a thought is significant. The transitions also contribute to the informal nature of the lectures with their frequent asides and polemical remarks, which the conventions of written prose scarcely allow. In these and other ways Heidegger the teacher is revealed.

In his intellectual development this book proves to be something of a turning point. During the late 'thirties and into the 'forties Heidegger was deeply involved with the thought of Nietzsche. It seemed to him necessary to come to grips with Nietzsche's absolutizing of the will as a culmination of Western metaphysics. By the time of the lectures here translated, it is clear that Nietzsche's thinking has been absorbed, "first found, and then lost," as he puts it. The difficulty of first finding and then losing Nietzsche causes him to recommend to his students that "they postpone reading Nietzsche for the time being, and first study Aristotle for ten to fifteen years." In the second half of the present volume, accordingly, we hear nothing further of Nietzsche's doctrine of the will to power or eternal recurrence. To discover what thinking is we are instead led back to the origins of Greek thinking before Aristotle. It is clear that the ideas which have preoccupied him in Germany's chaotic decades between 1930 and 1950 are gradually being replaced by the themes of the 'fifties and 'sixties.

These themes are frequently suggested in the present volume, even adumbrated, but not really developed. The one most noticeable is the nature of language, which has come to hold the center of his attention till the present and has received its fullest treatment in the book *Unterwegs zur Sprache*, 1959 (to appear later in this translation series). To be sure, Heidegger has long before this reflected on the mysterious nature of language in its relation to thinking and Being. But in the present lectures one can note progress toward the conception of language as that sphere in which man can dwell aright and make clear to himself who he is. Here Heidegger is more directly concerned with the way language relates to thinking and its response to the call of thought. Later he will make language itself the focus of his reflections and meditations. In this sense *What Is Called Thinking?* is a signpost on Heidegger's way.

The other theme increasingly to capture his attention is the nature of modern science and technology. It will doubtless shock the American reader to learn in these lectures that "science does not think." Even when such a reader remembers that the term "science" for Europeans includes history, literature, and philosophy as well as the natural sciences, he will still be affronted. He has probably suspected that the "later" Heidegger is anti-science and mystical and this assertion by Heidegger is likely to confirm his opinion. But if he continues to read with sufficient thoughtfulness, he will note much later in this book that "science does not think in the way thinkers think." In a certain sense then Heidegger is deliberately trying to shock such a reader as he was his students. No doubt this is an aspect of his pedagogical method, though his assertion has a more important purpose. Those who are acquainted with his later essays on science and technology will be hesitant to accept the impression that he is anti-science or that he is necessarily pessimistic about present developments. It certainly seems so but things are seldom what they seem in this man's writings.

If "the most thought-provoking thing about our thought-provoking age" is "that we are still not thinking," it has always been thus since the early Greeks. As he makes clear in this volume, Heidegger is neither pessimistic nor optimistic about the times in which we live. It is only that the nature of our technological age requires thinking more than earlier ages, for modern man conceives himself prepared to take dominion over the earth and his capacities for good and ill are vastly augmented.

Organized knowledge, that is, the natural and humanistic sciences, is not on a lower level than thinking as Heidegger understands it. Moreover, the sciences are more and more determining the character of contemporary reality. They spring from an authentic source in our Western heritage, for *techné* was for the Greeks a species of knowledge and in its own way a disclosure of truth and Being. Its predominance in our time calls for another kind of response, namely thinking, which stems from a different source than *techné* but also Greek. At all events in the present work Heidegger is not directly concerned with the nature of science, but with the nature of thinking, which he conceives to be quite another matter.

What is it that Heidegger does call thinking? It is important to say first of all what he does not call thinking. Thinking is, in the first place, not what we call having an opinion or a notion. Second, it is not representing or having an idea (*vorstellen*) about something or a state of affairs. This is an important negation for Heidegger, which he dealt with at greater length in "Conversations on a Country Path about Thinking" in *Discourse on Thinking* (Harper & Row, 1965). Third, thinking is not ratiocination, developing a chain of premises which lead to a valid conclusion. Lastly, it is not conceptual or systematic in the sense favored by the German idealistic tradition, the concept or *Begriff* believed by Hegel to be thinking *par excellence*.

Heidegger is, however, not denying the importance of these conceptions of thinking. He is hardly a "nothing but" kind of philosopher. Opining, representing, reasoning, conceiving—all have their place and function; they are more useful and necessary in most respects than is thinking as he understands it. These accustomed ways of grasping thinking, as he remarks in this book, are so stubborn "because they have their own truth." There is always a struggle to advance a new way of seeing things because customary ways and preconceptions about it stand in the way. The situation is similar to learning a foreign language: forgetting our mother tongue is the chief difficulty.

Furthermore, Heidegger makes no claim that thinking can produce knowledge as do the sciences, nor can it promote usable practical wisdom, solve any cosmic riddles, or endow us directly with the power to act. There is no salvation to be found in it. In all these ways it is clearly inferior to the sciences and to all these activities which commonly pass for thinking. Nevertheless, thinking in his sense does have its own importance and relevance. Heidegger is clearly working toward a theory of the independent role of a kind of thinking that is at once poetic and philosophic. Like many other Continental thinkers today, he wants to insist on a new conception of philosophy as an autonomous inquiry.

For Heidegger thinking is a response on our part to a call which issues from the nature of things, from Being itself. To be able to think does not wholly depend on our will and wish, though much does depend on whether we prepare ourselves to hear that call to think when it comes and respond to it in the appropriate manner. Thinking is determined by that which is to be thought as well as by him who thinks. It involves not only man's receptivity to Being but also Being's receptivity to man. The history and situation of man in a given age often covers up the nature of reality and renders it impossible to receive the message of Being.

Thinking is not so much an act as a way of living or dwelling—as we in America would put it, a way of life. It is a remembering who we are as human beings and where we belong. It is a gathering and focusing of our whole selves on what lies before us and a taking to heart and mind these particular things before us in order to discover in them their essential nature and truth. Learning how to think can obviously aid us in this discovery. Heidegger's conception of truth as the revealing of what is concealed, in distinction to the theory of truth as correctness or correspondence, is probably his most seminal thought and philosophy's essential task, as he sees it. The nature of reality and of man is both hidden and revealed; it both appears and withdraws from view, not in turn but concomitantly. Only the thinking that is truly involved, patient, and disciplined by long practice can come to know either the hidden or disclosed character of truth.

The final lecture in this volume, which parallels the last chapter in *Introduction to Metaphysics*, brings out most clearly—more clearly in my judgment than did the earlier

Intro. to Metaph., Ch. 6?

book—Heidegger's central intuitions about the nature of thinking. It represents his attempt to translate the famous saying of Parmenides about the relation of saying and thinking to Being. What Heidegger is here suggesting is that thinking is a concrete seeing and saying of the way the world is. Man is an integral part of this world and can realize it by asking questions of it, profound and naïve questions, and by waiting "even a whole lifetime" for the disclosures that may come. Thinking is unlike any other act insofar as it is an act at all. It is a calling in more than one sense of that richly evocative word. Thinking defines the nature of being human and the more thoughtless we are, the less human we are.

Yet thinking is inherent in man as a being-in-the-world. Hence learning to think is as much a discovery of our own nature as it is a discovery of the nature of Being. Every doctrine of man's nature, as he tells us in these lectures, is at one and the same time a doctrine of Being. And every doctrine of Being is by the same token a doctrine of human nature. That is to say, the relatedness of man to Being is so integral that inquiry into one involves of necessity the other, too.

This book closes with a question, appropriately, since the title and indeed most of the lectures are an extended question. To this question no answer is given in the sense of a definition or description. Indeed Heidegger teaches that none can be given. As we learn in the opening sentence: "We come to know what thinking means when we ourselves try to think." To define thinking for someone else would be as hopeless as describing colors to the blind. Thinking is questioning and putting ourselves in question as much as the cherished opinions and inherited doctrines we have long taken for granted. Each must learn to do it for himself. Heidegger as teacher demonstrates and encourages his students to follow suit. The result of such questioning is not negative or skeptical. Despite diversions and asides, the course of these lectures advances Heidegger's theme in such a way that we learn a good deal about how to question rightly.

This intimate connection between thinking and questioning is central to everything Heidegger is trying to learn by these exercises in thinking. Putting in question is not primarily a method for him as it was for Descartes and for his teacher Husserl. At least it is not a method in the sense that one uses it as a preliminary to building up a body of doctrine after tearing down earlier systems. No, for Heidegger questioning is a way or path of thinking each one must clear for himself with no certain destination in mind. It might be likened to making a first path on skis through new-fallen snow or clearing a way for oneself through dense forest growth. Questioning and thinking are not a means to an end; they are self-justifying. To think is to be *underway*, a favorite word of crucial importance to Heidegger. His general question remains constant, namely the relation of human being and other beings to Being as such; but the way changes frequently since he often gets onto bypaths and dead-ends. His persistence in holding to the question he has chosen to think about as well as his flexibility in approach to it are sources of admiration, even among the ranks of his detractors.

Since thinking and questioning are so nearly synonymous, it is difficult for critics and historians of thought to classify and "locate" him in the tradition. In Germany he is sometimes held to be a continuator of Hegel or Nietzsche. Or often he is thought to be a modern follower of Parmenides or Heraclitus. Despite his great love for the Greeks and his familiarity with Western philosophic thought, I believe it is a fundamental mistake to read Heidegger as a follower of this or that previous thinker. He seems to me to have no basic dependence on any predecessors, not even his own previous thought. If his thinking is never carried on in disregard of the tradition, he is rarely satisfied with the conclusions of others nor, after a time, with his own. Close students of his well realize how far he has come since *Being and Time,* however they may divide on the question of whether there has been a decisive "turn" since that early work. Today, at age seventy-nine, he starts every morning afresh, without any secure base in past systems of thought and still dissatisfied with what he himself has worked out.

A future age may well consider his contribution to philosophy to be that of an initiator of new approaches and perspectives on our common inheritance, rather than any new content or doctrine. He seeks to press beyond systems and concepts—to live in the *meta* as he here suggests was the simple and therefore inexhaustible significance of Greek thought. The one aspect of that thought seized upon by the Christian Middle Ages and carried over into modern thought, fruitful as it has been, he believes to have reached an impasse today. The only way to go forward is to return to the origins and seek a new beginning.

The advance Heidegger wishes to make on the basis of Greek thought is to learn to think non-conceptually and non-systematically yet with rigor and strictness about the nature of Being. By so doing he hopes to avoid the subjectivity involved in separating human being and Being, subject and object. He desires a thinking that is at once receptive in the sense of a listening and attending to what things convey to us and active in the sense that we respond to their call. Only when we are really immersed in what is to be thought can we reveal truly the nature of anything no matter how commonplace it may be, and only then can we avoid our habitual ways of grasping it as it is for us, *i.e.,* subjectively.

The call of thought is thus the call to be attentive to things as they are, to let them be as they are, and to think them and ourselves together. This is, (of course,) difficult, all the more so as Heidegger believes in this man-centered age of ours. It is an age in which "we consider it quite in order that we cannot all follow the thought processes of modern theoretical physics. But to learn the thinking of thinkers is essentially more difficult, not because that thinking is still more involved but because it is simple." Nevertheless, if we persist in attempting to master the handicraft of thinking, it is not impossible. Heidegger is persuaded that man is naturally inclined to think and Being desires to be thought truly.

To offer a translation of a Heideggerian work requires a measure of courage, perhaps better named rashness. The reasons are clearly stated in the present volume. A translation is necessarily an interpretation, according to him, and also every genuine thinking is ambiguous in its very nature. "Multiplicity of meanings is the element in which thought must move in order to be strict thought," he tells his students. Or again, to move within language is like moving "on the billowing waters of an ocean." Heidegger revels in the ambiguity of the German language and in the multiple meanings of the words he chooses. He thinks poetically, all the more the older he becomes. Translators can never be sure in a given case which of these meanings Heidegger wishes to predominate. One can, of course, use two or more English words for a single German term, and this we have frequently done.

It gradually becomes clear to a translator, however, that Heidegger rarely abandons the idiomatic sense of a German word, no matter how technical or terminological its overtones. He has great respect for the common idiom, though none at all for the commonness of thoughtless usage. Most of his words retain as much as possible of their root meanings in their Greek, Latin, or Old German origins. Hence, we have tried to stick to Anglo-Saxon equivalents where we could, and to keep uppermost the simple, non-technical sense of what he is trying to say. This way it is easier for the philosophically sophisticated reader to supply the contemporary technical connotations of these words, and for the layman in philosophy not to miss the essential message of this book.

Though Heidegger was extremely helpful in answering my questions about the meaning of a term, a sentence, or a whole passage, Fred Wieck and I would not claim that we have caught the intended emphasis in every case. This may well be the first Heidegger translation in English to be worked out in close cooperation with the author. But it does not pretend to be an authorized translation. Martin Heidegger does not know English well enough for that. However, we do believe that it is as close to the author's intentions as our own limitations in understanding and the requirements of readable English allow. If it remains, nonetheless, an interpretation, we trust that it is one which is faithful to the spirit and substance of the original.

PART

ONE

PART

ONE

LECTURE

I

------◆------

We come to know what it means to think when we ourselves try to think. If the attempt is to be successful, we must be ready to learn thinking.

As soon as we allow ourselves to become involved in such learning, we have admitted that we are not yet capable of thinking.

Yet man is called the being who can think, and rightly so. Man is the rational animal. Reason, *ratio*, evolves in thinking. Being the rational animal, man must be capable of thinking if he really wants to. Still, it may be that man wants to think, but can't. Perhaps he wants too much when he wants to think, and so can do too little. Man can think in the sense that he possesses the possibility to do so. This possibility alone, however, is no guarantee to us that we are capable of thinking. For we are capable of doing only what we are inclined to do. And again, we truly incline only toward something that in turn inclines toward us, toward our essential being, by appealing to our essential being as the keeper who holds us in our essential being. What keeps us in our essential nature holds us only so long, however, as we for our part keep holding on to what holds us. And we keep holding on to it by not letting it out of our memory. Memory is the gathering of thought. Thought of what?

Thought of what holds us, in that we give it thought precisely because It remains what must be thought about. Thought has the gift of thinking back, a gift given because we incline toward it. Only when we are so inclined toward what in itself is to be thought about, only then are we capable of thinking.

In order to be capable of thinking, we need to learn it first. What is learning? Man learns when he disposes everything he does so that it answers to whatever essentials are addressed to him at any given moment. We learn to think by giving our mind to what there is to think about.

What is essential in a friend, for example, is what we call "friendly." In the same sense we now call "thought-provoking" what in itself is to be thought about. Everything thought-provoking *gives* us to think. But it always gives that gift just so far as the thought-provoking matter already *is* intrinsically what must be thought about. From now on, we will call "most thought-provoking" what remains to be thought about always, because it is at the beginning, before all else. What is most thought-provoking? How does it show itself in our thought-provoking time?

Most thought-provoking is that we are still not thinking —not even yet, although the state of the world is becoming constantly more thought-provoking. True, this course of events seems to demand rather that man should act, without delay, instead of making speeches at conferences and international conventions and never getting beyond proposing ideas on what ought to be, and how it ought to be done. What is lacking, then, is action, not thought.

And yet—it could be that prevailing man has for centuries now acted too much and thought too little. But how dare anyone assert today that we are still not thinking, today when there is everywhere a lively and constantly more audible interest in philosophy, when almost everybody claims to know what philosophy is all about! Philosophers are *the* thinkers *par excellence*. They are called thinkers precisely because thinking properly takes place in philosophy.

Nobody will deny that there is an interest in philosophy today. But—is there anything at all left today in which man does not take an interest, in the sense in which he understands "interest"?

Interest, *interesse*, means to be among and in the midst of things, or to be at the center of a thing and to stay with it. But today's interest accepts as valid only what is interesting. And interesting is the sort of thing that can freely be regarded as indifferent the next moment, and be displaced by something else, which then concerns us just as little as what went before. Many people today take the view that they are doing great honor to something by finding it interesting. The truth is that such an opinion has already relegated the interesting thing to the ranks of what is indifferent and soon boring.

It is no evidence of any readiness to think that people show an interest in philosophy. There is, of course, serious preoccupation everywhere with philosophy and its problems. The learned world is expending commendable efforts in the investigation of the history of philosophy. These are useful and worthy tasks, and only the best talents are good enough for them, especially when they present to us models of great thinking. But even if we have devoted many years to the intensive study of the treatises and writings of the great thinkers, that fact is still no guarantee that we ourselves are thinking, or even are ready to learn thinking. On the contrary—preoccupation with philosophy more than anything else may give us the stubborn illusion that we are thinking just because we are incessantly "philosophizing."

Even so, it remains strange, and seems presumptuous, to assert that what is most thought-provoking in our thought-provoking time is that we are still not thinking. Accordingly, we must prove the assertion. Even more advisable is first to explain it. For it could be that the demand for a proof collapses as soon as enough light is shed on what the assertion says. It runs:

Most thought-provoking in our thought-provoking time is that we are still not thinking.

It has been suggested earlier how the term "thought-provoking" is to be understood. Thought-provoking is what gives us to think. Let us look at it closely, and from the start allow each word its proper weight. Some things are food for thought in themselves, intrinsically, so to speak innately. And some things make an appeal to us to give them thought, to turn toward them in thought: to think them.

What is thought-provoking, what gives us to think, is then not anything that we determine, not anything that only we are instituting, only we are proposing. According to our assertion, what of itself gives us most to think about, what is most thought-provoking, is this—that we are still not thinking.

This now means: We have still not come face to face, have not yet come under the sway of what intrinsically desires to be thought about in an essential sense. Presumably the reason is that we human beings do not yet sufficiently reach out and turn toward what desires to be thought. If so, the fact that we are still not thinking would merely be a slowness, a delay in thinking or, at most, a neglect on man's part. Such human tardiness could then be cured in human ways by the appropriate measures. Human neglect would give us food for thought—but only in passing. The fact that we are still not thinking would be thought-provoking, of course, but being a momentary and curable condition of modern man, it could never be called the one most thought-provoking matter. Yet that is what we call it, and we suggest thereby the following: that we are still not thinking is by no means only because man does not yet turn sufficiently toward that which, by origin and innately, wants to be thought about since in its essence its remains what must be thought about. Rather, that we are still not thinking stems from the fact that the thing itself that must be thought about turns away from man, has turned away long ago.

We will want to know at once when that event took place. Even before that, we will ask still more urgently how we could possibly know of any such event. And finally, the problems which here lie in wait come rushing at us when we add still further: that which really gives us food for thought did not turn away from man at some time or other which can be fixed in history—no, what really must be thought keeps itself turned away from man since the beginning.

On the other hand, in our era man has always thought in some way; in fact, man has thought the profoundest thoughts, and entrusted them to memory. By thinking in that way he did and does remain related to what must be thought. And yet man is not capable of really thinking as long as that which must be thought about, withdraws.

If we, as we are here and now, will not be taken in by empty talk, we must retort that everything said so far is an unbroken chain of hollow assertions, and state besides that what has been presented here has nothing to do with scientific knowledge.

It will be well to maintain as long as possible such a defensive attitude toward what has been said: only in that attitude do we keep the distance needed for a quick running dash by which one or the other of us may succeed in making the leap into thinking. For it is true that what was said so far, and the entire discussion that is to follow, have nothing to do with scientific knowledge, especially not if the discussion itself is to be a thinking. This situation is grounded in

the fact that science itself does not think, and cannot think
—which is its good fortune, here meaning the assurance
of its own appointed course. Science does not think. This is
a shocking statement. Let the statement be shocking, even
though we immediately add the supplementary statement
that nonetheless science always and in its own fashion has
to do with thinking. That fashion, however, is genuine and
consequently fruitful only after the gulf has become visible
that lies between thinking and the sciences, lies there un-
bridgeably. There is no bridge here—only the leap. Hence
there is nothing but mischief in all the makeshift ties and
asses' bridges by which men today would set up a comfortable commerce between thinking and the sciences.
Hence we, those of us who come from the sciences, must
endure what is shocking and strange about thinking—
assuming we are ready to learn thinking. To learn means to
make everything we do answer to whatever essentials address themselves to us at the given moment. In order to be
capable of doing so, we must get underway. It is important
above all that on the way on which we set out when we
learn to think, we do not deceive ourselves and rashly by-
pass the pressing questions; on the contrary, we must allow
ourselves to become involved in questions that seek what no
inventiveness can find. Especially we moderns can learn
only if we always unlearn at the same time. Applied to the
matter before us : we can learn thinking only if we radically
unlearn what thinking has been traditionally. To do that,
we must at the same time come to know it.

We said: man still does not think, and this because what
must be thought about turns away from him; by no means
only because man does not sufficiently reach out and turn
to what is to be thought.

What must be thought about, turns away from man. It
withdraws from him. But how can we have the least knowledge of something that withdraws from the beginning,

how can we even give it a name? Whatever withdraws, refuses arrival. But—withdrawing is not nothing. Withdrawal is an event. In fact, what withdraws may even concern and claim man more essentially than anything present that strikes and touches him. Being struck by actuality is what we like to regard as constitutive of the actuality of the actual. However, in being struck by what is actual, man may be debarred precisely from what concerns and touches him —touches him in the surely mysterious way of escaping him by its withdrawal. The event of withdrawal could be what is most present in all our present, and so infinitely exceed the actuality of everything actual.

What withdraws from us, draws us along by its very withdrawal, whether or not we become aware of it immediately, or at all. Once we are drawn into the withdrawal, we are drawing toward what draws, attracts us by its withdrawal. And once we, being so attracted, are drawing toward what draws us, our essential nature already bears the stamp of "drawing toward." As we are drawing toward what withdraws, we ourselves are pointers pointing toward it. We are who we are by pointing in that direction—not like an incidental adjunct but as follows: this "drawing toward" is in itself an essential and therefore constant pointing toward what withdraws. To say "drawing toward" is to say "pointing toward what withdraws."

To the extent that man *is* drawing that way, he *points* toward what withdraws. *As* he is pointing that way, man *is* the pointer. Man here is not first of all man, and then also occasionally someone who points. No: drawn into what withdraws, drawing toward it and thus pointing into the withdrawal, man first *is* man. His essential nature lies in being such a pointer. Something which in itself, by its essential nature, is pointing, we call a sign. As he draws toward what withdraws, man is a sign. But since this sign points toward what draws *away*, it points, not so much at what draws away as into the withdrawal. The sign stays without interpretation.

In a draft to one of his hymns, Hoelderlin writes:

> "We are a sign that is not read."

He continues with these two lines:

> "We feel no pain, we almost have
> Lost our tongue in foreign lands."

The several drafts of that hymn—besides bearing such titles as "The Serpent," "The Sign," "The Nymph"—also include the title "Mnemosyne." This Greek word may be translated: Memory. And since the Greek word is feminine, we break no rules if we translate "Dame Memory."

For Hoelderlin uses the Greek word *Mnemosyne* as the name of a Titaness. According to the myth, she is the daughter of Heaven and Earth. Myth means the telling word. For the Greeks, to tell is to lay bare and make appear —both the appearance and that which has its essence in the appearance, its epiphany. *Mythos* is what has its essence in its telling—what is apparent in the unconcealedness of its appeal. The *mythos* is that appeal of foremost and radical concern to all human beings which makes man think of what appears, what is in being. *Logos* says the same; *mythos* and *logos* are not, as our current historians of philosophy claim, placed into opposition by philosophy as such; on the contrary, the early Greek thinkers (Parmenides, fragment 8) are precisely the ones to use *mythos* and *logos* in the same sense. *Mythos* and *logos* become separated and opposed only at the point where neither *mythos* nor *logos* can keep to its original nature. In Plato's work, this separation has already taken place. Historians and philologists, by virtue of a prejudice which modern rationalism adopted from Platonism, imagine that *mythos* was destroyed by *logos*. But nothing religious is ever destroyed by logic; it is destroyed only by the God's withdrawal.

Mnemosyne, daughter of Heaven and Earth, bride of Zeus, in nine nights becomes the mother of the nine Muses. Drama and music, dance and poetry are of the womb of Mnemosyne, Dame Memory. It is plain that the word means something else than merely the psychologically demonstrable ability to retain a mental representation, an idea, of something which is past. Memory—from Latin *memor*, mindful—has in mind something that is in the mind, thought. But when it is the name of the Mother of the Muses, "Memory" does not mean just any thought of anything that can be thought. Memory is the gathering and convergence of thought upon what everywhere demands to be thought about first of all. Memory is the gathering of recollection, thinking back. It safely keeps and keeps concealed within it that to which at each given time thought must be given before all else, in everything that essentially is, everything that appeals to us as what has being and has been in being. Memory, Mother of the Muses—the thinking back to what is to be thought is the source and ground of poesy. This is why poesy is the water that at times flows backward toward the source, toward thinking as a thinking back, a recollection. Surely, as long as we take the view that logic gives us any information about what thinking is, we shall never be able to think how much all poesy rests upon thinking back, recollection. Poetry wells up only from devoted thought thinking back, recollecting.

Under the heading *Mnemosyne*, Hoelderlin says:

"We are a sign that is not read . . ."

We? Who? We the men of today, of a "today" that has lasted since long ago and will still last for a long time, so long that no calendar in history can give its measure. In the same hymn, "Mnemosyne," it says: "Long is/The time"—the time in which we are a sign, a sign that is not read. And this, that we are a sign, a sign that is not read—does this not give enough food for thought? What the poet says in

these words, and those that follow, may have a part in showing us what is most thought-provoking: precisely what the
assertion about our thought-provoking time attempts to
think of. And that assertion, provided only we explain it
properly, may throw some little light for us upon the poet's
word; Hoelderlin's word, in turn, because it is a word of
poesy, may summon us with a larger appeal, and hence
greater allure, upon a way of thought that tracks in thought
what is most thought-provoking. Even so, it is as yet obscure what purpose this reference to the words of Hoelderlin is supposed to serve. It is still questionable with what
right we, by way of an attempt to think, make mention of a
poet, this poet in particular. And it is also still unclear
upon what ground, and within what limits, our reference
to the poetic must remain.

Summary and Transition

By way of this series of lectures, we are attempting to learn
thinking. The way is long. We dare take only a few steps.
If all goes well, they will take us to the foothills of thought.
But they will take us to places which we must explore to
reach the point where only the leap will help further. The
leap alone takes us into the neighborhood where thinking
resides. We therefore shall take a few practice leaps right
at the start, though we won't notice it at once, nor need to.

In contrast to a steady progress, where we move un-
awares from one thing to the next and everything remains
alike, the leap takes us abruptly to where everything is different, so different that it strikes us as strange. Abrupt
means the sudden sheer descent or rise that marks the
chasm's edge. Though we may not founder in such a leap,
what the leap takes us to will confound us.

It is quite in order, then, that we receive notice from the
very start of what will confound us. But all would not be

well if the strangeness were due only to the fact that you, the listeners, are not yet listening closely enough. If that were the case, you would be bound to overlook completely the strangeness which lies in the matter itself. The matter of thinking is always confounding—all the more in proportion as we keep clear of prejudice. To keep clear of prejudice, we must be ready and willing to listen. Such readiness allows us to surmount the boundaries in which all customary views are confined, and to reach a more open territory. In order to encourage such readiness, I shall insert here some transitional remarks, which will also apply to all subsequent lectures.

In universities especially, the danger is still very great that we misunderstand what we hear of thinking, particularly if the immediate subject of the discussion is scientific. Is there any place compelling us more forcibly to rack our brains than the research and training institutions pursuing scientific labors? Now everyone admits unreservedly that the arts and the sciences are totally different from each other, though in official oratory they are still mentioned jointly. But if a distinction is made between thinking and the sciences, and the two are contrasted, that is immediately considered a disparagement of science. There is the fear even that thinking might open hostilities against the sciences, and becloud the seriousness and spoil the joy of scientific work.

But even if those fears were justified, which is emphatically not the case, it would still be both tactless and tasteless to take a stand against science upon the very rostrum that serves scientific education. Tact alone ought to prevent all polemics here. But there is another consideration as well. Any kind of polemics fails from the outset to assume the attitude of thinking. The opponent's role is not the thinking role. Thinking is thinking only when it pursues whatever speaks *for* a subject. Everything said here defensively is always intended exclusively to protect the subject. When we speak of the sciences as we pursue our way, we shall be speaking not against but for them, for clarity concerning their essential nature. This alone implies our conviction that the sciences are in themselves positively essential. However, their essence is frankly of a different sort from what our universities today still fondly imagine it to be. In any case, we still seem afraid of facing the exciting fact that today's sciences belong in the realm of the essence of modern technology, and nowhere else. Be it noted that I am saying "in the realm of the *essence* of technology," and not simply "in technology." A fog still surrounds the essence of modern science. That fog, however, is not produced by individual investigators and scholars in the sciences. It is not produced by man at all. It arises from the region of what is most thought-provoking—that we are still not thinking; none of us, including me who speaks to you, me first of all.

This is why we are here attempting to learn thinking. We are all on the way together, and are not reproving each other. To learn means to make everything we do answer to whatever essentials address themselves to us at a given time. Depending on the kind of essentials, depending on the realm from which they address us, the answer and with it the kind of learning differs.

A cabinetmaker's apprentice, someone who is learning to build cabinets and the like, will serve as an example. His learning is not mere practice, to gain facility in the use of tools. Nor does he merely gather knowledge about the customary forms of the things he is to build. If he is to become a true cabinetmaker, he makes himself answer and respond above all to the different kinds of wood and to the shapes slumbering within wood—to wood as it enters into man's dwelling with all the hidden riches of its nature. In fact, this relatedness to wood is what maintains the whole craft. Without that relatedness, the craft will never be anything but empty busywork, any occupation with it will be determined exclusively by business concerns. Every handicraft, all human dealings are constantly in that danger. The writing of poetry is no more exempt from it than is thinking.

Whether or not a cabinetmaker's apprentice, while he is learning, will come to respond to wood and wooden things, depends obviously on the presence of some teacher who can make the apprentice comprehend.

True. Teaching is even more difficult than learning. We know that; but we rarely think about it. And why is teaching more difficult than learning? Not because the teacher must have a larger store of information, and have it always ready. Teaching is more difficult than learning because what teaching calls for is this: to let learn. The real teacher, in fact, lets nothing else be learned than—learning. His conduct, therefore, often produces the impression that we properly learn nothing from him, if by "learning" we now suddenly understand merely the procurement of useful information. The teacher is ahead of his apprentices in this alone, that he has still far more to learn than they—he has to learn to let them learn. The teacher must be capable of being more teachable than the apprentices. The teacher is far less assured of his ground than those who learn are of theirs. If the relation between the teacher and the taught is genuine, therefore, there is never a place in it for the authority of the know-it-all or the authoritative sway of the official. It still is an exalted matter, then, to become a teacher—which is something else entirely than becoming a famous professor. That nobody wants any longer to become a teacher today, when all things are downgraded and graded from below (for instance, from business), is presumably because the matter is exalted, because of its altitude. And presumably this disinclination is linked to that

most thought-provoking matter which gives us to think.
We must keep our eyes fixed firmly on the true relation
between teacher and taught—if indeed learning is to arise
in the course of these lectures.

We are trying to learn thinking. Perhaps thinking, too,
is just something like building a cabinet. At any rate, it is a
craft, a "handicraft." "Craft" literally means the strength
and skill in our hands. The hand is a peculiar thing. In the
common view, the hand is part of our bodily organism.
But the hand's essence can never be determined, or explained, by its being an organ which can grasp. Apes, too,
have organs that can grasp, but they do not have hands.
The hand is infinitely different from all grasping organs—
paws, claws, or fangs—different by an abyss of essence.
Only a being who can speak, that is, think, can have hands
and can be handy in achieving works of handicraft.

But the craft of the hand is richer than we commonly
imagine. The hand does not only grasp and catch, or push
and pull. The hand reaches and extends, receives and wel-
comes—and not just things: the hand extends itself, and
receives its own welcome in the hands of others. The hand
holds. The hand carries. The hand designs and signs,
presumably because man is a sign. Two hands fold into one,
a gesture meant to carry man into the great oneness. The
hand is all this, and this is the true handicraft. Everything
is rooted here that is commonly known as handicraft, and
commonly we go no further. But the hand's gestures run
everywhere through language, in their most perfect purity
precisely when man speaks by being silent. And only when
man speaks, does he think—not the other way around, as
metaphysics still believes. Every motion of the hand in every
one of its works carries itself through the element of thinking, every bearing of the hand bears itself in that element.
All the work of the hand is rooted in thinking. Therefore,
thinking itself is man's simplest, and for that reason hard-

est, handiwork, if it would be accomplished at its proper time.

We must learn thinking because our being able to think, and even gifted for it, is still no guarantee that we are capable of thinking. To be capable, we must before all else incline toward what addresses itself to thought—and that is that which of itself gives food for thought. What gives us this gift, the gift of what must properly be thought about, is what we call most thought-provoking.

Our answer to the question what the most thought-provoking thing might be is the assertion: most thought-provoking for our thought-provoking time is that we are still not thinking.

The reason is never exclusively or primarily that we men do not sufficiently reach out and turn toward what properly gives food for thought; the reason is that this most thought-provoking thing turns away from us, in fact has long since turned away from man.

And what withdraws in such a manner, keeps and develops its own, incomparable nearness.

Once we are so related and drawn to what withdraws, we are drawing into what withdraws, into the enigmatic and therefore mutable nearness of its appeal. Whenever man is properly drawing that way, he is thinking—even though he may still be far away from what withdraws, even though the withdrawal may remain as veiled as ever. All through his life and right into his death, Socrates did nothing else than place himself into this draft, this current, and maintain himself in it. This is why he is the purest thinker of the West. This is why he wrote nothing. For anyone who begins to write out of thoughtfulness must inevitably be like those people who run to seek refuge from any draft too strong for them. An as yet hidden history still keeps the secret why all great Western thinkers after Socrates, with all their greatness, had to be such fugitives.

Thinking has entered into literature; and literature has decided the fate of Western science which, by way of the *doctrina* of the Middle Ages, became the *scientia* of modern times. In this form all the sciences have leapt from the womb of philosophy, in a twofold manner. The sciences come out of philosophy, because they have to part with her. And now that they are so apart they can never again, by their own power as sciences, make the leap back into the source from whence they have sprung. Henceforth they are remanded to a realm of being where only thinking can find them, provided thinking is capable of doing what is its own to do.

When man is drawing into what withdraws, he points into what withdraws. As we are drawing that way we are a sign, a pointer. But we are pointing then at something which has not, not yet, been transposed into the language of our speech. We are a sign that is not read.

In his draft for the hymn "Mnemosyne" (Memory), Hoelderlin says:

> "We are a sign that is not read,
> We feel no pain, we almost have
> Lost our tongue in foreign lands."

And so, on our way toward thinking, we hear a word of poesy. But the question to what end and with what right, upon what ground and within what limits, our attempt to think allows itself to get involved in a dialogue with poesy, let alone with the poetry of this poet—this question, which is inescapable, we can discuss only after we ourselves have taken the path of thinking.

LECTURE
II

How shall we ever be able to think about the oft-named relation between thought and poesy, so long as we do not
know what is called thinking and what calls for thinking,
and therefore cannot think about what poesy is? We modern men presumably have not the slightest notion how
thoughtfully the Greeks experienced their lofty poetry,
their works of art—no, not experienced, but let them stand
there in the presence of their radiant appearance.

Yet this much might be clear to us right now: we are
not dragging Hoelderlin's words into our lecture merely
as a quotation from the realm of the poetic statement which
will enliven and beautify the dry progress of thinking. To
do so would be to debase the poetic word. Its statement rests
on its own truth. This truth is called beauty. Beauty is a
fateful gift of the essence of truth, and here truth means
the disclosure of what keeps itself concealed. The beautiful
is not what pleases, but what falls within that fateful gift
of truth which comes to be when that which is eternally
non-apparent and therefore invisible attains its most radi-
antly apparent appearance. We are compelled to let the
poetic word stand in *its* truth, in beauty. And that does not
exclude but on the contrary includes that we think the
poetic word.

When we appropriate Hoelderlin's word specifically for the realm of thought, we must of course be careful not to equate unthinkingly Hoelderlin's poetic statement with what we are starting out to think about and call "most thought-provoking." What is stated poetically, and what is stated in thought, are never identical; but there are times when they are the same—those times when the gulf separating poesy and thinking is a clean and decisive cleft. This can occur when poesy is lofty, and thinking profound. Hoelderlin understood the matter well, as we gather from the two stanzas of the poem entitled

Socrates and Alcibiades

"Why, holy Socrates, must you always adore
    This young man? Is there nothing greater than he?
        Why do you look on him
        Lovingly, as on a god?"

(The second stanza gives the answer:)

"Who has most deeply thought, loves what is most alive,
    Who has looked at the world, understands youth at its
        height,
        And wise men in the end
        Often incline to beauty."

We are concerned here with the line "Who has most deeply thought, loves what is most alive." It is all too easy in this line to overlook the truly telling and thus sustaining words, the verbs. To notice the verb, we now stress the line in a different way that will sound unfamiliar to the common hearer:

"Who has most deeply *thought*, *loves* what is most alive."

Standing in the closest vicinity, the two verbs "thought" and "loves" form the center of the line. Inclination reposes

in thinking. Curious rationalism which bases love on thinking! And an unpleasant kind of thinking which is about to
become sentimental! But there is no trace of any of this in
that line. What the line tells we can fathom only when we
are capable of thinking. And that is why we ask: What is
called thinking—and what does call for it?

We shall never learn what "is called" swimming, for
example, or what it "calls for," by reading a treatise on
swimming. Only the leap into the river tells us what is
called swimming. The question "What is called thinking?"
can never be answered by proposing a definition of the concept *thinking*, and then diligently explaining what is contained in that definition. In what follows, we shall not
think *about* what thinking is. We remain outside that mere
reflection which makes thinking its object. Great thinkers,
first Kant and then Hegel, have understood the fruitlessness
of such reflection. That is why they had to attempt to reflect
their way out of such reflection. How far they got, and
where it took them, are questions that will give us much to
think about at the proper juncture along our way. In the
West, thought about thinking has flourished as "logic."
Logic has gathered special knowledge concerning a special
kind of thinking. This knowledge concerning logic has been
made scientifically fruitful only quite recently, in a special
science that calls itself "logistics." It is the most specialized
of all specialized sciences. In many places, above all in the
Anglo-Saxon countries, logistics is today considered the
only possible form of strict philosophy, because its result
and procedures yield an assured profit for the construction
of the technological universe. In America and elsewhere,
logistics as the only proper philosophy of the future is thus
beginning today to seize power over the spirit. Now that
logistics is in some suitable way joining forces with modern
psychology and psychoanalysis, and with sociology, the
power-structure of future philosophy is reaching perfec-

tion. But this conformation is in no way of man's making, or within his power. Rather, these disciplines are in fateful submission to a power which comes from far away, and for which the Greek words ποίησις (poesy) and τέχνη (technology) may still be the appropriate names, provided they signify for us, who are thinking, That which gives food for thought.

Summary and Transition

The Summary and Transition at the end of Lecture 1 concerned three things : the relatedness of thinking to science; the relation between teaching and learning; and thinking as a handicraft.

We refrain from repeating the three points, and will try instead to clarify a few questions and reflections concerning that transition which have been brought up from various sides.

When we decide to look for the essential nature of contemporary science in the essence of modern technology, this approach posits science as something in the highest sense worthy of thought. The significance of science is ranked higher here than in the traditional views which see in science merely a phenomenon of human civilization.

For the essence of technology is not anything human. The essence of technology is above all not anything technological. The essence of technology lies in what from the beginning and before all else gives food for thought. It might then be advisable, at least for the time being, to talk and write less about technology, and give more thought to where its essence lies, so that we might first find a way to it. The essence of technology pervades our existence in a way which we have barely noticed so far. This is why in the preceding lecture, precisely at a juncture which almost demanded a reference to the technological world, we kept silent about technology. It now turns out that the demands made here on you, the students, have been excessive for the beginning of our journey. We have called thinking the handicraft *par excellence.*

Thinking guides and sustains every gesture of the hand.

We were talking about the cabinetmaker's craft. It could be objected that even the village cabinetmaker works with machines nowadays. It could be pointed out that today gigantic industrial factories have risen alongside the craftsmen's workshops, and have in fact been there for quite some time. Inside the factories, working men pull the same lever day and night for eight to ten hours at a stretch, and working women push the same button. The point is correct. But in this case, and in this form, it has not yet been thought out. The objection falls flat, because it has heard only half of what the discussion has to say about handicraft. We chose the cabinetmaker's craft as our example, assuming it would not occur to anybody that this choice indicated any expectation that the state of our planet could in the foreseeable future, or indeed ever, be changed back into a rustic idyll. The cabinetmaker's craft was proposed as an example for our thinking because the common usage of the word "craft" is restricted to human activities of that sort. However—it was specifically noted that what maintains and sustains even this handicraft is not the mere manipulation of tools, but the relatedness to wood. But where in the manipulations of the industrial worker is there any relatedness to such things as the shapes slumbering within wood? This is the question you were meant to run up against, though not to stop there. For as long as we raise questions only in this way, we are still questioning from the standpoint of the familiar and previously customary handicraft.

What about the lever? What about the button which the worker manipulates? Levers and buttons have long existed even on the workbenches of an old-fashioned craftsman's shop. But the lever and buttons in the manipulations of the industrial worker belong to a machine. And where does the machine, such as a power generator, belong? Modern technology is not constituted by, and does not consist in, the installation of electric motors and turbines and similar machinery; that sort of thing can on the contrary be erected only to the extent to which the essence of modern technology has already assumed dominion. Our age is not a technological age because it is the age of the machine; it is an age of the machine because it is the technological age. But so long as the essence of technology does not closely concern us, in our thought, we shall never be able to know what the machine is. We shall not be able to tell what it is to which the industrial worker's hand is related. We shall not be able to make out what kind of manual work, of handicraft, these manipulations are. And yet—merely to be able to ask such questions, we must already have caught sight of what is commonly meant by handicraft in the light of its essential references. Neither the industrial workman nor the engineers, let alone the factory proprietor and least of all the state, can know at all where modern man "lives" when he stands in some relatedness or other to the machine and machine parts. None of us know as yet what handicraft modern man in the technological world must carry on, must carry on even if he is not a worker in the sense of the worker at the machine. Neither Hegel nor Marx could know it yet, nor could they ask why their thinking, too, still had to move in the shadow of the essential nature of technology; and so they never achieved the freedom to grasp and adequately think about this nature. Important as the economic, social, political, moral, and even religious questions may be which are being discussed in connection with technological labor or handicraft, none of them reach to the core of the matter. That matter keeps itself hidden in the still unthought nature of the way in which anything that is under the dominion of technology has any being at all. And that such matters have remained unthought is indeed first of all due to the fact that the will to action, which here means the will to make and be effective, has overrun and crushed thought.

Some of us may recall the statement of the first lecture that so far man has acted too much, and thought too little. However, the reason why thought has failed to appear is not only, and not primarily, that man has cultivated thought too little, but because what is to be thought about, what properly gives food for thought, has long been withdrawing. Because this withdrawal prevails, that for which the craft of technological manipulation reaches out remains hidden. This withdrawal is what properly gives food for thought, what is most thought-provoking. Perhaps we notice now more readily that this most thought-provoking thing, in which the essence of modern technology also keeps itself hidden, appeals to us constantly and everywhere; indeed, what is most thought-provoking is even closer to us than the most palpable closeness of our everyday handiwork —and yet it withdraws. Hence our need and necessity first of all to hear the appeal of what is most thought-provoking. But if we are to perceive what gives us food for thought, we must for our part get underway to learn thinking.

Whether, by way of this learning though never by means of it, we shall attain relatedness to what is most thought-provoking, is something altogether out of the hands of those who practice the craft of thinking.

What we can do in our present case, or anyway can learn, is to listen closely. To learn listening, too, is the common concern of student and teacher. No one is to be blamed, then, if he is not yet capable of listening. But by the same token you must concede that the teacher's attempt may go wrong and that, where he happens not to go wrong, he must often resign himself to the fact that he can not lay before you in each instance all that should be stated.

On the other hand, you will make close listening essentially easier for yourselves if you will rid yourselves in time of a habit which I shall call "one-track thinking." The dominion of this manner of perception is so vast today that our eyes can barely encompass it. The expression "one-track" has been chosen on purpose. Track has to do with rails, and rails with technology. We would be making matters too easy for ourselves if we simply took the view that the dominion of one-track thinking has grown out of human laziness. This one-track thinking, which is becoming ever more widespread in various shapes, is one of those unsuspected and inconspicuous forms, mentioned earlier, in which the essence of technology assumes dominion— because that essence wills and therefore needs absolute univocity.

In the preceding lecture it was said that Socrates was the purest thinker of the West, while those who followed had to run for shelter. There comes the horrified retort: "But what about Plato, Augustine, Thomas Aquinas, Leibniz, Kant, Nietzsche? Dare we reduce these thinkers so much in comparison with Socrates?" But our questioner has failed to hear what was also said: all great Western thinkers after Socrates "with all their greatness." Someone, then, could still be the purest thinker without being one of the greatest. That would give us here much to think about. For that reason, the remark about Socrates began with the words: "An as yet hidden history still keeps the secret why all great thinkers after Socrates, with all their greatness . . ."

We hear something of Socrates, the purest thinker—we fail to hear the rest, and then along the one track of something half-heard we travel on right into being horrified at such one-sidedly dogmatic statements. Things are similar with the conclusion of the second lecture. There we said that our way remains outside that mere reflection which makes thinking its object. How can anyone make such a statement after he has for two solid hours spoken of nothing else but thinking? However, to reflect on thinking, and to trace thinking in thought, are perhaps not altogether the same. We must give thought to what reflection means.

LECTURE
III

———◆———

When we attempt to learn what is called thinking and what calls for thinking, are we not getting lost in the reflection that thinks on thinking? Yet all along our way a steady light is cast on thinking. This light, however, is not introduced by the lamp of reflection. It issues from thinking itself, and only from there. Thinking has this enigmatic property, that it itself is brought to its own light—though only if and only as long as it is thinking, and keeps clear of persisting in ratiocination about *ratio*.

Thinking is thinking when it answers to what is most thought-provoking. In our thought-provoking time, what is most thought-provoking shows itself in the fact that we are still not thinking. For the moment, what this sentence says is no more than an assertion. It has the form of a statement, and this statement we shall now deal with. We shall for now discuss two points: first the tone of the assertion, and then its character as a statement.

The assertion claims: What is most thought-provoking in our thought-provoking time is that we are still not thinking.

What we call thought-provoking in the condition of someone gravely ill, for example, is that it gives us cause for worry. We call thought-provoking what is dark, threat-

ening, and gloomy, and generally what is adverse. When
we say "thought-provoking," we usually have in mind
immediately something injurious, that is, negative. Accordingly, a statement that speaks of a thought-provoking
time, and even of what is most thought-provoking in it,
is from the start tuned in a negative key. It has in view only
the adverse and somber traits of the age. It sticks exclusively
to those phenomena that are good for nothing and promote
every form of nothingness—the nihilistic phenomena. And
it necessarily assumes that at the core of those phenomena
there is a lack—according to our proposition, lack of
thought.

This tune is familiar to us all *ad nauseam* from the standard appraisals of the present age. A generation ago it was
"The Decline of the West." Today we speak of "loss of
center." People everywhere trace and record the decay, the
destruction, the imminent annihilation of the world. We
are surrounded by a special breed of reportorial novels that
do nothing but wallow in such deterioration and depression.
On the one hand, that sort of literature is much easier to
produce than to say something that is essential and truly
thought out; but on the other hand it is already getting tire-
some. The world, men find, is not just out of joint but tum-
bling away into the nothingness of absurdity. Nietzsche,
who from his supreme peak saw far ahead of it all, as early
as the eighteen-eighties had for it the simple, because
thoughtful, words: "The wasteland grows." It means, the
devastation is growing wider. Devastation is more than
destruction. Devastation is more unearthly than destruction.
Destruction only sweeps aside all that has grown up or been
built up so far; but devastation blocks all future growth
and prevents all building. Devastation is more unearthly
than mere destruction. Mere destruction sweeps aside all
things including even nothingness, while devastation on
the contrary establishes and spreads everything that blocks

and prevents. The African Sahara is only one kind of waste-land. The devastation of the earth can easily go hand in hand with a guaranteed supreme living standard for man, and just as easily with the organized establishment of a uniform state of happiness for all men. Devastation can be the same as both, and can haunt us everywhere in the most unearthly way—by keeping itself hidden. Devastation does not just mean a slow sinking into the sands. Devastation is the high-velocity expulsion of Mnemosyne. The words, "the wasteland grows," come from another realm than the current appraisals of our age. Nietzsche said "the waste-land grows" nearly three quarters of a century ago. And he added, "Woe to him who hides wastelands within."

Now it seems as though our assertion, that "what is most thought-provoking in our thought-provoking time is that we are still not thinking," were part of the same chorus of voices that disparage modern Europe as sick, and our age as on the decline.

Let us listen more closely! The assertion says, what is most thought-provoking is that we are still not thinking. The assertion says neither that we are no longer thinking, nor does it say roundly that we are not thinking at all. The words "still not," spoken thoughtfully, suggest that we are already on our way toward thinking, presumably from a great distance, not only on our way toward thinking as a conduct some day to be practiced, but on our way *within* thinking, on the way of thinking.

Our assertion, then, casts a bright ray of hope into that obfuscation which seems not only to oppress the world from somewhere, but which men are almost dragging in by force. It is true that our assertion calls the present age the thought-provoking age. What we have in mind with this word—and without any disparaging overtones—is that which gives us food for thought, which is what wants to be thought about. What is thought-provoking, so understood, need in no way be what causes us worry or even perturbs us. Joyful things, too, and beautiful and mysterious and gracious things give us food for thought. These things may even be more thought-provoking than all the rest which we otherwise, and usually without much thought, call "thought-provoking." These things will give us food for thought, if only we do not reject the gift by regarding everything that is joyful, beautiful, and gracious as the kind of thing which should be left to feeling and experience, and kept out of the winds of thought. Only after we have let ourselves become involved with the mysterious and gracious things as those which properly give food for thought, only then can we take thought also of how we should regard the malice of evil.

What is most thought-provoking, then, could be something lofty, perhaps even the highest thing there is for man, provided man still is the being who *is* insofar as he thinks, thinks in that thought appeals to him because his essential nature consists in memory, the gathering of thought. And what is most thought-provoking—especially when it is man's highest concern—may well be also what is most dangerous. Or do we imagine that a man could even in small ways encounter the essence of truth, the essence of beauty, the essence of grace—without danger?

Therefore, when our assertion speaks of the thought-provoking age and of what is most thought-provoking in it, it is in no way tuned to a key of melancholy and despair. It is not drifting blindly toward the worst. It is not pessimistic. But neither is the assertion optimistic. It does not intend to offer quick comfort through artificially hopeful prospects of the best. But what alternative remains? Indecision between the two? Indifference? These least of all. For all indecision always feeds only on those matters between which it remains undecided. Even the man who believes his judgments to be beyond pessimism and optimism (or on their hither side), still always takes his bearings from optimism and pessimism, and guides himself by a mere variant of indifference. But pessimism and optimism both, together with the indifference and its variants which they support, stem from a peculiar relatedness of man to what we call history. This relatedness is difficult to grasp in its peculiarity—not because it is situated far away, but because it is by now habitual to us. Our assertion, too, patently stems from a relatedness to the history and situation of man. What is the nature of that relatedness? This brings us to the second point about our assertion to which we must give attention.

Summary and Transition

After our transitional remarks on science, on learning, and on hand and handicraft, we returned to our theme. A reference to one-track thinking provided the transition. One-track thinking is something else than mere one-sided thinking; it has a greater reach and a loftier origin. In the present discourse concerning one-sided and one-track thinking, the word "thinking" means as much as "having views." One might say, for instance: "I think it will snow tonight." But he who speaks that way is not thinking, he just has views on something. We must be very careful, however, not to regard this "viewing" as insignificant. All our daily life and all we do moves within what we have in view, and necessarily so. Even the sciences stay within it. And how is it one-sided? Is it not one of science's highest principles to explore its objects from as many sides as possible, even from all sides? Where is the one-sidedness in that? It lies precisely in the sphere of scientific exploration. Historical science may thoroughly explore a period, for instance, in every possible respect, and yet never explore what history is. It cannot do so, scientifically. By way of history, a man will never find out what history is; no more than a mathematician can show by way of mathematics—by means of his science, that is, and ultimately by mathematical formulae—what mathematics is. The essence of their sphere—history, art, poetry, language, nature, man, God —remains inaccessible to the sciences. At the same time, however, the sciences would constantly fall into the void if they did not operate within these spheres. The essence of the spheres I have named is the concern of thinking. As the sciences *qua* sciences have no access to this concern, it must be said that they are not thinking. Once this is put in words, it tends to sound at first as though thinking fancied itself superior to the sciences. Such arrogance, if and where it exists, would be unjustified; thinking always knows essentially less than the sciences precisely because it operates where it could think the essence of history, art, nature, language—and yet is still not capable of it. The sciences are fully entitled to their name, which means fields of knowledge, because they have infinitely more knowledge than thinking does. And yet there is another side in every science which that science as such can never reach: the essential nature and origin of its sphere, the essence and essential origin of the manner of knowing which it cultivates, and other things besides. The sciences remain of necessity on the one side. In this sense they are one-sided, but in such a way that the other side nonetheless always appears as well. The sciences' one-sidedness retains its own many-sidedness. But that many-sidedness may expand to such proportions that the one-sidedness on which it is based no longer catches our eye. And when man no longer sees the one side as *one* side, he has lost sight of the other side as well. What sets the two sides apart, what lies between them, is covered up, so to speak. Everything is leveled to one level. Our minds hold views on all and everything, and view all things in the identical way. Today every newspaper, every illustrated magazine, and every radio program offers all things in the identical way to uniform views. The subjects of science and the concern of thinking are dealt with in the identical manner. However, it would be a disastrous error for us to take the view that the mention of such phenomena merely served to characterize or even criticize our present age. We should fall victim to a disastrous self-deception if we were to take the view that a haughty contempt is all that is needed to let us escape from the imperceptible power of the uniformly one-sided view. On the contrary, the point is to discern what weird, unearthly things are here in the making. The one-sided view, which nowhere pays attention any longer to the essence of things, has puffed itself up into an all-sidedness which in turn is masked so as to look harmless and natural. But this all-sided view which deals in all and everything with equal uniformity and mindlessness, is only a preparation for what is really going on. For it is only on the plane of the one-sided uniform view that one-track thinking takes its start. It reduces everything to a univocity of concepts and specifications the precision of which not only corresponds to, but has the same essential origin as, the precision of technological process. For the moment, we need to keep in mind only that one-track thinking is not co-extensive with the one-sided view, but rather is building on it even while transforming it. A symptom, at first sight quite superficial, of the growing power of one-track thinking is the increase everywhere of designations consisting of abbreviations of words, or combinations of their initials. Presumably no one here has ever given serious thought to what has already come to pass when you, instead of *University*, simply say "U." "U"—that is like "movie." True, the moving picture theater continues to be different from the academy of the sciences. Still, the designation "U" is not accidental, let alone harmless. It may even be in order that you go in and out of the "U" and study "phy. sci." But the question remains *what kind* of order is heralded here in the spreading of this kind of language. Perhaps it is an order into which we are drawn, and to which we are abandoned, by That which withdraws from us.

And that is what we call most thought-provoking. According to our assertion, it expresses itself in that we are still not thinking.

The assertion seems to be tuned in a negative and pessimistic key. However, "thought-provoking" here means what gives food for thought. Most thought-provoking is not only what gives most food for thought, in the sense that it makes the greatest demands on our thinking; most thought-provoking is what inherently gathers and keeps within itself the greatest riches of what is thought-worthy and memorable. Our assertion says that we are still not thinking. This "still not" contains a peculiar reference to something still to come, of which we absolutely do not know whether it will come to us. This "still not" is of a unique kind, which refuses to be equated with other kinds. For example, we can say, around midnight, that the sun has still not come up. We can say the same thing in the early dawn. The "still not" in each case is different. But, it will be objected, it is different here only regarding the time span, the number of hours that pass between midnight and dawn; while the daily rising of the sun is certain. Certain in what sense? Perchance in the scientific sense? But since Copernicus, science no longer recognizes sunrises and sunsets. Scientifically, it has been unequivocally established that these things are illusions of the senses. By the common assumption of the customary view, this "still not" concerning the rising sun retains its truth at midnight and at dawn; but this truth can never be scientifically established, for the simple reason that the daily morning expectation of the sun is of a nature that has no room for scientific proofs. When

we wait for the sun to rise, we never do it on the strength
of scientific insight. It will be objected that men have become habituated to the regularity of these phenomena. As
though the habitual went without saying, as though it were
understood! As though there could be anything habitual
without habitation! As though we had ever given thought
to habitation! Now if even the coming and going of the sun
is such a rare and curious matter for us, how much more
mysterious will matters be in that realm where that which
must be thought withdraws from man and, at the same
time, in its withdrawal, comes to him.

This, and this alone, is why we say, then, that what gives
us most food for thought is that we are still not thinking.
This means: insofar as we *are* at all, we are already in a
relatedness to what gives food for thought. Even so, in our
thinking we have still not come to what is most thought-
provoking. Nor can we know by ourselves whether we will
get there. Accordingly, our assertion is not optimistic
either; nor does it hang suspended in indecision between
pessimism and optimism, for then it would have to reckon
with both and thereby basically adopt their ways of reckoning.

The key in which our assertion is tuned cannot, then, be
determined simply like that of an ordinary statement.
Therefore, it will be well to give thought not only to the
key note of our assertion, but also to its character as a
statement.

LECTURE
IV

First, the tone of our assertion is in no way negative, though it may easily seem so to an inattentive listener or reader. In general, the proposition does not express a disparaging attitude of any sort. The second point concerns the question whether the assertion is a statement. The way in which our assertion speaks can be adequately indicated only when we are able to give thought to what the assertion actually says. That possibility will at best present itself at the end of our lectures, or long afterward. It is much more likely that this most fortunate eventuality will still not come about. This is why we must even now pay attention to the question posed for us by the assertion when we consider the way in which it speaks, or how it speaks. By "way," or "how," we mean something other than manner or mode. "Way" here means melody, the ring and tone, which is not just a matter of how the saying sounds. The way or how of the saying is the tone from which and to which what is said is attuned. We suggest, then, that the two questions—concerning the "tone" of our assertion, and concerning its nature as a statement—hang together.

One can hardly deny, it seems, that the assertion, which speaks of our thought-provoking time and of what in it is most thought-provoking, is a judgment on the present age.

How do things stand with such judgments on the present? They describe the age as on the decline, for instance, as sick, decaying, stricken with "loss of center." What is decisive about such judgments, however, is not that they evaluate everything negatively, but that they evaluate at all. They determine the value, so to speak the price range into which the age belongs. Such appraisals are considered indispensable, but also unavoidable. Above all, they immediately create the impression of being in the right. Thus they promptly win the approval of the many, at least for whatever time is allotted to such judgments. That time now grows steadily shorter. If people today tend once again to be more in agreement with Spengler's proposition about the decline of the West, it is (along with various superficial reasons) because Spengler's proposition is only the negative, though correct, consequence of Nietzsche's words: "The wasteland grows." We emphasized that these are words issuing from thought. They are true words.

Still, it appears that judgments on the age which issue from other sources are just as much in the right. Indeed they are, in that they are correct, since they take their direction from, and conform to, facts which can be brought in by the carload for documentation, and can be documented by adroitly selected quotations from learned authors. An idea is called correct when it conforms to its object. Such correctness in the forming of an idea has long since been equated with truth—that is, we determine the nature of truth by the conformity of the idea. If I say: "Today is Friday," the statement is correct, because it directs and conforms the idea to the sequence of days in the week, and arrives at this day. To judge is to form correct ideas. When we judge something—as when we say: "That tree is blossoming"—our idea must maintain the direction toward the object, the blossoming tree. But this maintenance of direction is constantly beset by the possibility that we do not attain the direction, or else we lose it. The idea does not thereby become undirected, but incorrect with reference to the object. Putting it more specifically, to judge is to form ideas correctly, and therefore also possibly incorrectly. In order now to show in what way our assertion about the present age has the nature of a statement, we must demonstrate more clearly how things stand with judgments, that is, with the forming of correct and incorrect ideas. As soon as we think that matter through properly, we are caught up in this question: what is this anyway—to form an idea, a representation?

Is there anyone among us who does not know what it is to form an idea? When we form an idea of something—of a text if we are philologists, a work of art if we are art historians, a combustion process if we are chemists—we have a representational idea of those objects. Where do we have those ideas? We have them in our head. We have them in our consciousness. We have them in our soul. We have the ideas inside ourselves, these ideas of objects.

Now it is true that a few centuries ago philosophy began to meddle in the matter, and by now has made it questionable whether the ideas inside ourselves answer to any reality at all outside ourselves. Some say yes; others, no; still others say that the matter cannot be decided anyway, all one can say is that the world—that is, here, the totality of what is real—is there insofar as we have an idea of it. "The world is my idea." In this sentence Schopenhauer has summed up the thought of recent philosophy. Schopenhauer must be mentioned here, because his main work, *The World as Will and Idea*, ever since its publication in 1818, has most persistently determined the whole tone of all of nineteenth- and twentieth-century thought—even where this is not immediately obvious, and even where Schopenhauer's statement is opposed. We forget too easily that a thinker is more essentially effective where he is opposed than where he finds agreement. Even Nietzsche had to pass through a head-on confrontation with Schopenhauer; and despite the fact that his understanding of the will was the opposite of Schopenhauer's, Nietzsche held fast to Schopenhauer's axiom: "The world is my idea." Schopenhauer himself says the following about this axiom (in Chapter One, Volume Two of his main work) :

" 'The world is my idea'—this, like the axioms of Euclid, is a statement whose truth must be recognized by anyone who understands it; though not (a statement) of the kind that anyone understands who hears it.—To have made us conscious of this statement, and to have connected it with the problem of the relation of the ideal to the real, i.e., the relation of the world in the head to the world outside the head—this, in addition to the problem of moral freedom, is what gives its distinctive character to the philosophy of the moderns. For only after thousands of years of trials with purely objective philosophizing did we discover that, among the many things that make the world so enigmatic and so thought-provoking, the closest and most immediate thing is this: however immeasurable and massive the world may be, yet its existence hangs by one single thin thread: and that is the given individual consciousness in which it is constituted."

Given this discord among philosophers concerning what the forming of ideas is in essence, there is patently just one way out into the open. We leave the field of philosophical speculation behind us, and first of all investigate carefully and scientifically how matters really stand with the ideas that occur in living beings, especially in men and animals. Such investigations are among the concerns of psychology. Psychology is today a well-established and already extensive science, and its importance is growing year by year.

But we here leave to one side the findings of psychology concerning what it calls "ideas"; not because these findings are incorrect, let alone unimportant, but because they are scientific findings. For, being scientific statements, they are already operating in a realm which for psychology, too, must remain on that other side of which we spoke before. It is no cause for wonder, then, that within psychology it never becomes clear in any way what it is to which ideas are attributed and referred—to wit, the organism of living things, consciousness, the soul, the unconscious and all the depths and strata in which the realm of psychology is articulated. Here everything remains in question; and yet, the scientific findings are correct.

If we nonetheless leave science aside now in dealing with the question what it is to form ideas, we do so not in the proud delusion that we have all the answers, but out of discretion inspired by a lack of knowledge.

The word "idea" comes from the Greek εἴδω which means to see, face, meet, be face-to-face.

We stand outside of science. Instead we stand before a tree in bloom, for example—and the tree stands before us. The tree faces us. The tree and we meet one another, as the tree stands there and we stand face to face with it. As we are in this relation of one to the other and before the other, the tree and we *are*. This face-to-face meeting is not, then, one of these "ideas" buzzing about in our heads. Let us stop here for a moment, as we would to catch our breath before and after a leap. For that is what we *are* now, men who have leapt, out of the familiar realm of science and even, as we shall see, out of the realm of philosophy. And where have we leapt? Perhaps into an abyss? No! Rather, onto some firm soil. Some? No! But on that soil upon which we live and die, if we are honest with ourselves. A curious, indeed unearthly thing that we must first leap onto the soil on which we really stand. When anything so curious as this leap becomes necessary, something must have happened that gives food for thought. Judged scientifically, of course, it remains the most inconsequential thing on earth that each of us has at some time stood facing a tree in bloom. After all, what of it? We come and stand facing a tree, before it, and the tree faces, meets us. Which one is meeting here? The tree, or we? Or both? Or neither? We come and stand—just as we are, and not merely with our head or our consciousness—facing the tree in bloom, and the tree faces, meets us as the tree it is. Or did the tree anticipate us and come before us? Did the tree come first to stand and face us, so that we might come forward face-to-face with it?

What happens here, that the tree stands there to face us, and we come to stand face-to-face with the tree? Where does this presentation take place, when we stand face-to-face before a tree in bloom? Does it by any chance take place in our heads? Of course; many things may take place in our brain when we stand on a meadow and have standing before us a blossoming tree in all its radiance and fragrance —when we perceive it. In fact, we even have transforming and amplifying apparatus that can show the processes in our heads as brain currents, render them audible, and re-trace their course in curves. We can—of course! Is there anything modern man can not do? He even can be helpful now and then, with what he can do. And he is helping everywhere with the best intentions. Man can—probably none of us have as yet the least premonition of what man will soon be able to do scientifically. But—to stay with our example—while science records the brain currents, what becomes of the tree in bloom? What becomes of the meadow? What becomes of the man—not of the brain but of the man, who may die under our hands tomorrow and be lost to us, and who at one time came to our encounter? What becomes of the face-to-face, the meeting, the seeing, the forming of the idea, in which the tree presents itself and man comes to stand face-to-face with the tree?

When ideas are formed in this way, a variety of things happen presumably also in what is described as the sphere of consciousness and regarded as pertaining to the soul. But does the tree stand "in our consciousness," or does it stand on the meadow? Does the meadow lie in the soul, as experience, or is it spread out there on earth? Is the earth in our head? Or do we stand on the earth?

It will be said in rebuttal: What is the use of such questions concerning a state of affairs which everybody will in fairness admit immediately, since it is clear as day to all the world that we are standing on the earth and, in our example, face-to-face with a tree? But let us not slip too hastily into this admission, let us not accept and take this "clear as day" too lightly. For we shall forfeit everything before we know it, once the sciences of physics, physiology, and psychology, not to forget scientific philosophy, display the panoply of their documents and proofs, to explain to us that what we see and accept is properly not a tree but in reality a void, thinly sprinkled with electric charges here and there that race hither and yon at enormous speeds. It will not do to admit, just for the scientifically unguarded moments, so to speak, that, naturally, we are standing face to face with a tree in bloom, only to affirm the very next moment as equally obvious that this view, naturally, typifies only the naïve, because pre-scientific, comprehension of things. For with that affirmation we have conceded something whose consequences we have hardly considered, and that is: that those sciences do in fact decide what of the tree in bloom may or may not be considered valid reality. Whence do the sciences—which necessarily are always in the dark about the origin of their own nature—derive the authority to pronounce such verdicts? Whence do the sciences derive the right to decide what man's place is, and to offer themselves as the standard that justifies such decisions? And they will do so just as soon as we tolerate, if only by our silence, that our standing face-to-face with the tree is no more than a pre-scientifically intended relation to something we still happen to call "tree." In truth, we are today rather inclined to favor a supposedly superior physical and physiological knowledge, and to drop the blooming tree.

When we think through what this is, that a tree in bloom presents itself to us so that we can come and stand face-to-face with it, the thing that matters first and foremost, and finally, is not to drop the tree in bloom, but for once let it stand where it stands. Why do we say "finally"? Because to this day, thought has never let the tree stand where it stands.

Still, the scientific study of the history of Western thought reports that Aristotle, judged by his theory of knowledge, was a realist. A realist is a man who affirms the existence and knowability of the external world. Indeed, it never occurred to Aristotle to deny the existence of the external world. Nor did it ever occur to Plato, any more than to Heraclitus or Parmenides. But neither did these thinkers ever specifically affirm the presence of the external world, let alone prove it.

Summary and Transition

We got into the question: what is this anyway—to form an idea? For the moment, I need not remark on the steps that brought us to this point. But we must always keep reminding ourselves of the way we are trying to walk. We mark it with the question: what is called thinking—what does call for thinking? By way of this question, we get into the question: what is this—to form a representational idea?

It could be supposed that the forming of thoughts and the forming of ideas may well be one and the same thing. The prospect opens up on this possibility, that the traditional nature of thinking has received its shape from repre-

sentations, that thoughts are a kind of representational
idea. That is true. But at the same time it remains obscure
how this shaping of the nature of traditional thinking takes
place. The source of the event remains obscure. And it remains obscure finally what all this signifies for our attempt
to learn thinking. We understand, of course, and consider it
the most obvious thing in the world, when someone says, "I
think the matter is such and such," and with it has in mind,
"I have such and such an idea of the matter." It clearly follows that to think is to form ideas. Yet all the relations
called up by this statement remain in the shadow. Basically
they are still inaccessible to us. Let us be honest with ourselves: the essential nature of thinking, the essential origin
of thinking, the essential possibilities of thinking that are
comprehended in that origin—they are all strange to us,
and by that very fact they are what gives us food for
thought before all else and always; which is not surprising
if the assertion remains true that what is most thought-
provoking in our thought-provoking age is that we are still
not thinking. But that assertion says also that we are on the
way, in thought, to the essence of thought. We are underway, and by such ways have taken our departure from a
thinking whose essential nature seems to lie in the forming
of ideas and to exhaust itself in that. Our own manner of
thinking still feeds on the traditional nature of thinking,
the forming of representational ideas. But we still do not
think inasmuch as we have not yet entered into that nature
which is proper to thinking, and which is still reserved,
withheld from us. We are still not in the reality of thought.
The real nature of thought might show itself, however, at
that very point where it once withdrew, if only we will pay
heed to this withdrawal, if only we will not insist, confused by logic, that we already know perfectly well what
thinking is. The real nature of thought might reveal itself
to us if we remain underway. We are underway. What does

that mean? We are still *inter vias*, between divergent ways. Nothing has been decided yet about which is the one inevitable, and hence perhaps the only, way. Underway, then —we must give particularly close attention to that stretch of way on which we are putting our feet. We meant to be attentive to it from the first lecture on. But it seems that we have still not been fully in earnest about that intention, with all its consequences. As a marker on our path of thought, we quoted the words of the West's last thinker, Nietzsche. He said: "The wasteland grows . . ." We explicitly contrasted these words with other statements about the present age, not only because of their special content, but above all in view of the manner in which they speak. For they speak in terms of the kind of way on which Nietzsche's thinking proceeds. That way, however, comes from far away, and at every point gives evidence of that origin. Nietzsche neither made nor chose his way himself, no more than any other thinker ever did. He is sent on his way. And so the words "The wasteland grows . . ." become a word on the way. This means: the tale that these words tells does not just throw light on the stretch of the way and its surroundings. The tale itself traces and clears the way. The words are never a mere statement about the modern age, which could be freely taken out of Nietzsche's exposition. Still less are they an expression of Nietzsche's inner experiences. To say it more completely: Nietzsche's words are such an expression, too, of course, if we conceive of language in its most superficial character—as people usually do—and take the view that it presses the internal outward into the external and thus is—expression. But even if we do not take his words "The wasteland grows" in this obvious manner, the mere mention of Nietzsche's name brings rushing to our minds a flood of ideas—ideas which today less than ever offer assurance that they point toward what this thinker really thought.

But because those words "The wasteland grows . . ." will be seen in a very special light as we proceed, while the name "Nietzsche" threatens to become merely a label of ignorance and misinterpretation; and because the allusion in our lecture to these words has led to a variety of rash and mistaken interim opinions, we shall here reach ahead and anticipate some of what is to follow. In order not to confuse the course of our presentation, we shall be content with an allusion.

LECTURE
V

What is called thinking? We must guard against the blind
urge to snatch at a quick answer in the form of a formula.
We must stay with the question. We must pay attention to
the way in which the question asks: what is called thinking,
what does call for thinking?

"You just wait—I'll teach you what we call obedience!"
a mother might say to her boy who won't come home. Does
she promise him a definition of obedience? No. Or is she
going to give him a lecture? No again, if she is a proper
mother. Rather, she will convey to him what obedience is.
Or better, the other way around: she will bring him to
obey. Her success will be more lasting the less she scolds
him; it will be easier, the more directly she can get him to
listen—not just condescend to listen, but listen in such a
way that he can no longer stop wanting to do it. And why?
Because his ears have been opened and he now can hear
what is in accord with his nature. Learning, then, cannot
be brought about by scolding. Even so, a man who teaches
must at times grow noisy. In fact, he may have to scream
and scream, although the aim is to make his students learn
so quiet a thing as thinking. Nietzsche, most quiet and
shiest of men, knew of this necessity. He endured the agony
of having to scream. In a decade when the world at large

still knew nothing of world wars, when faith in "progress" was virtually *the* religion of the civilized peoples and nations, Nietzsche screamed out into the world: "The wasteland grows . . ." He thus put the question to his fellowmen and above all to himself: "Must one smash their ears before they learn to listen with their eyes? Must one clatter like kettledrums and preachers of repentance?"* But riddle upon riddle! What was once the scream "The wasteland grows . . . ," now threatens to turn into chatter. The threat of this perversion is part of what gives us food for thought. The threat is that perhaps this most thoughtful thought will today, and still more tomorrow, become suddenly no more than a platitude, and as platitude spread and circulate. This fashion of talking platitudes is at work in that endless profusion of books describing the state of the world today. They describe what by its nature is indescribable, because it lends itself to being thought about only in a thinking that is a kind of appeal, a call—and therefore must at times become a scream. Script easily smothers the scream, especially if the script exhausts itself in description, and aims to keep men's imagination busy by supplying it constantly with new matter. The burden of thought is swallowed up in the written script, unless the writing is capable of remaining, even in the script itself, a progress of thinking, a way. About the time when the words "The wasteland grows . . ." were born, Nietzsche wrote in his notebook (GW XIV, p. 229, Aphorism 464 of 1885): "A man for whom nearly all books have become superficial, who has kept faith in only a few people of the past that they have had depth enough—not to write what they knew." But Nietzsche had to scream. For him, there was no other way to do it than by writing. That written scream of Nietzsche's thought is the book which he entitled *Thus Spoke Zarathustra*. Its first three parts were written

* *Thus Spoke Zarathustra, Prologue, 5.*

and published between 1883 and 1884. The fourth part was written in 1884/85, but printed only for his closest circle of friends. That work thinks this thinker's one and only thought: the thought of the eternal recurrence of the same. Every thinker thinks one only thought. Here, too, thinking differs essentially from science. The researcher needs constantly new discoveries and inspirations, else science will bog down and fall into error. The thinker needs one thought only. And for the thinker the difficulty is to hold fast to this one only thought as the one and only thing that he must think; to think this One as the Same; and to tell of this Same in the fitting manner. But we speak of the Same in the manner that befits it only if we always say the same about it, in such a way that we ourselves are claimed by the Self-Same. The limitlessness of the Same is the sharpest limit set to thinking. The thinker Nietzsche hints at this hidden fittingness of thought by giving his *Thus Spoke Zarathustra* a subtitle which runs: *A Book for Everyone and No One*. "For Everyone"—that does not mean for everybody as just anybody; "For Everyone" means for each man as man, for each man each time his essential nature becomes for him an object worthy of his thought. "And No One"—that means: for none among these men prevailing everywhere who merely intoxicate themselves with isolated fragments and passages from the book and then blindly stumble about in its language, instead of getting underway on its way of thinking, and thus becoming first of all questionable to themselves. *Thus Spoke Zarathustra: A Book for Everyone and No One*. In what an unearthly fashion this subtitle has come true in the seventy years since the book first appeared—only in the exactly opposite sense. It has become a book for everyman, and not one thinker has appeared who could stand up to this book's basic thought, and to its darkness. In this book, its fourth and final part, Nietzsche wrote the words: "The wasteland grows . . ."

Into those words, Nietzsche put all he knew. They are the title of a poem Nietzsche wrote when he was "most distant from cloudy, damp, melancholy Old Europe." Complete, the words run: "The wasteland grows: woe to him who hides wastelands within!" Woe to whom? Was Nietzsche thinking of himself? What if he had known that it was his own thought which would first have to bring about a devastation in whose midst, in another day and from other sources, oases would rise here and there and springs well up? What if he had known that he himself had to be a precursor, a transition, pointing before and behind, leading and rebuffing, and therefore everywhere ambiguous, even in the manner and in the sense of the transition? All thoughtful thought argues that this is so, as Nietzsche himself knew and often put into enigmatic words. This is why every thoughtful converse with him is constantly carried into other dimensions. This is also why all formulas and labels fail in a special sense, and fall silent, in the face of Nietzsche's thought. We do not mean to say that Nietzsche's thought is no more than a game with images and symbols which can be called off any time. The thought of his thinking is as unambiguous as anything can be; but this unambiguity is many-chambered, in chambers that adjoin, join, and fuse. One reason is that all the themes of Western thought, though all of them transmuted, fatefully gather together in Nietzsche's thinking. This is why they refuse to be historically computed and accounted for. Only a dialogue can answer, then, to Nietzsche's thought which is a transition—a dialogue whose own way is preparing a transition. In such a transition, Nietzsche's thought as a whole must, of course, take its place on the one side which the transition leaves behind to move to the other. This transition, different in its reach and kind, is not here under discussion. The remark is merely to suggest that the transition, more far-reaching and different in kind, must of course leave the one side, but for that very reason cannot pass it over in the sense of disregarding it. In the course of the transition, Nietzsche's thought, the entire thought of the West is appropriated in its proper truth. That truth, however, is by no means obvious. Regarding Nietzsche, we limit ourselves to rendering visible the one essential that casts its light ahead as Nietzsche's thinking proceeds on its way. It will indicate to us at what turn of his thinking the words were spoken: "The wasteland grows; woe to him who hides wastelands within!"

But to encounter Nietzsche's thinking at all, we must first find it. Only when we have succeeded in finding it may we try to lose again what that thinking has thought. And this, to lose, is harder than to find; because "to lose" in such a case does not just mean to drop something, leave it behind, abandon it. "To lose" here means to make ourselves truly free of that which Nietzsche's thinking has thought. And that can be done only in this way, that we, on our own accord and in our memory, set Nietzsche's thought free into the freedom of its own essential substance—and so leave it at that place where it by its nature belongs. Nietzsche knew of these relations of discovery, finding, and losing. All along his way, he must have known of them with ever greater clarity. For only thus can it be understood that at the end of his way he could tell it with an unearthly clarity. What he still had to say in this respect is written on one of those scraps of paper which Nietzsche sent out to his friends about the time when he collapsed in the street (January 4, 1889) and succumbed to madness. These scraps are sometimes called "epistles of delusion." Understood medically, scientifically, that classification is correct. For the purposes of thinking, it remains inadequate.

One of these scraps is addressed to the Dane Georg Brandes, who had delivered the first public lectures on Nietzsche at Copenhagen, in 1888.

"Postmark Torino, 4 Jan 89

"To my friend Georg!

After you had discovered me, it was no trick to find me : the difficulty now is to lose me. . . .

The Crucified."

Did Nietzsche know that through him something was put into words that can never be lost again? Something that cannot be lost again to thinking, something to which thinking must forever come back again the more thoughtful it becomes? He knew it. For the decisive sentence, introduced by a colon, is no longer addressed only to the recipient of the paper. The sentence expresses a universal fateful state of affairs. "The difficulty now is to lose me. . . ." Now, and for all men, and henceforth. This is why we read the sentence, even the whole content of the paper, as if it were addressed to us. Now that we can look over the sixty-three years passed since then, at least in their broad outlines, we must admit, of course, that there remains for us the further difficulty first of all to find Nietzsche, though he has been discovered, that is, though it is known that the event of this thinker's thinking has taken place. In fact, this known fact only increases the danger that we shall not find Nietzsche, because we imagine we have already been relieved of the search. Let us not be deluded into the view that Nietzsche's thought has been found, just because there exists a Nietzsche literature that has been proliferating for the last fifty years. It is as though Nietzsche had foreseen this, too; it is not for nothing that he has Zarathustra say : "They all talk about me . . . but nobody gives me a thought." Thought can be given only where there is thinking. How are we to give thought to Nietzsche's thinking if we are still not thinking? Nietzsche's thinking, after all, does not contain just the extravagant views of an exceptional human being. This thinking puts into its own language that which is, more precisely, that which is still to be. For the "modern age" is in no way at an end. Rather, it is just entering the beginning of its presumably long-drawn-out consummation. And Nietzsche's thought? Part of what is thought-provoking is that Nietzsche's thought has still not been found. Part of what is most thought-provoking is that we are not in the least prepared truly to lose what is found, rather than merely pass it over and by-pass it. Bypassing of this sort is often done in an innocent form—by offering an overall exposition of Nietzsche's philosophy. As though there could be an exposition that is not necessarily, down in its remotest nook and cranny, an interpretation. As though any interpretation could escape the necessity of taking a stand or even, simply by its choice of starting point, of being an unspoken rejection and refutation. But no thinker can ever be overcome by our refuting him and stacking up around him a literature of refutation. What a thinker has thought can be mastered only if we refer everything in his thought that is still unthought back to its originary truth. Of course, the thoughtful dialogue with the thinker does not become any more comfortable that way; on the contrary, it turns into a disputation of rising acrimony. Meantime, however, Nietzsche goes on being bravely refuted. This industry, as we shall see, had early reached the point where thoughts were fabricated and ascribed to him which are the exact opposite of those he really thought, those in which his thinking finally consumed itself.

Summary and Transition

The way of our question "what is called thinking?" has brought us to the question: what is this anyway—to form an idea? So far, an answer has suggested itself only in vague outline: the forming of ideas could even be the uni-

versally prevailing basic characteristic of traditional thinking. Our own way derives from such thinking. It therefore
remains necessarily bound to a dialogue with traditional
thinking. And since our way is concerned with thinking
for the specific purpose of learning it, the dialogue must
discuss the nature of traditional thinking. But while such
thinking has already become aware that it is a kind of forming ideas, there is absolutely no assurance that traditional
thinking has ever given sufficient thought to the *essence* of
idea-forming, or even could do so. In any dialogue with
the nature of prevailing thinking, then, the *essence* of idea-
forming is probably the first thing that must be put into the
language of thinking. If we respond to that language, not
only do we come to know thinking in its historic nature
and destiny—we come to learn thinking itself.

The representative of traditional thinking who is closest
to us in time, and hence most stimulating to this discussion,
is Nietzsche. For his thought, in traditional language, tells
what *is*. But the oft-named matters of fact, the conditions,
the tendencies of the age always remain only the foreground of what is. Yet Nietzsche's language, too, speaks
only in the foreground, so long as we understand it exclusively in terms of the language of traditional thinking,
instead of listening for what remains unspoken in it. Accordingly, we gave ear from the start to a word of Nietzsche
which lets us hear something unspoken: "The wasteland
grows; woe to him who hides wastelands within!"

But it has become necessary to improve our ability to
listen. We shall do so with a suggestion that will turn us
more pointedly in the direction in which Nietzsche's
thought is striving. Nietzsche sees clearly that in the history
of Western man something is coming to an end: what until
now and long since has remained uncompleted. Nietzsche
sees the necessity to carry it to a completion. But completion does not mean here that a part is added which was

missing before; this completion does not make whole by patching; it makes whole by achieving at last *the wholeness* of the whole, by thus transforming what has been so far, in virtue of the whole.

But if we are to catch sight of even a fraction of these fateful relations, we must extricate ourselves again from the error into which we have fallen, that one can think through Nietzsche's thinking by dealing with it historically. That mistaken attitude feeds on the view that Nietzsche's thought can be put aside as something that is past and well refuted. People have no idea how difficult it is truly to lose that thought again—assuming it has been found.

But everything argues that it has not even been found yet. Accordingly, we must first search for it. And our suggestion concerning the direction of Nietzsche's own way is thus still a searching suggestion.

LECTURE
VI

With greater clarity than any man before him, Nietzsche saw the necessity of a change in the realm of essential thinking, and with this change the danger that conventional man will adhere with growing obstinacy to the trivial surface of his conventional nature, and acknowledge only the flatness of these flatlands as his proper habitation on earth. The danger is all the greater because it arises at a moment in history which Nietzsche was the first man to recognize clearly, and the only man so far to think through metaphysically in all its implications. It is the moment when man is about to assume dominion of the earth as a whole.

Nietzsche was the first man to raise the question: Is man, as he has been and still is, prepared to assume that dominion? If not, then what must happen to man as he is, so that he can make the earth "subject" to himself and thus fulfill the words of an old testament? Within the purview of his thinking, Nietzsche calls man as he has been till now "the last man." This is not to say that all human existence will end with the man so named. Rather, the last man is the man who is no longer able to look beyond himself, to rise above himself for once up to the level of his task, and undertake that task in a way that is essentially right. Man so far is incapable of it, because he has not yet come into his own full nature. Nietzsche declares that man's essential nature is not yet determined—it has neither been found nor been secured. This is why Nietzsche says: "Man is the as yet undetermined animal." The statement sounds strange. Yet it only puts into words what Western thought has thought of man from the beginning. Man is the rational animal. Through reason, man raises himself above the animal, but so that he must constantly look down upon the animal, subject it, master it. If we call animal characteristics "sensual," and take reason as non-sensual or supra-sensual, then man—the rational animal—appears as the sensual supra-sensual being. If we follow tradition and call the sensual "physical," then reason, the supra-sensual, is what goes beyond the sensual, the physical; in Greek, "beyond" is μετά; μετὰ τὰ φυσικά means beyond the physical, the sensual; the supra-sensual, in passing beyond the physical, is the metaphysical. Man conceived as the rational animal is the physical exceeding the physical; in short—in the nature of man as the rational animal, there is gathered the passing from the physical to the non-physical, the supraphysical: thus man himself is the metaphysical. But since for Nietzsche neither man's physical, sensual side—his body, nor man's non-sensual side—his reason, have been adequately conceived in their essential nature, man, in the prevailing definition, remains the as yet unconceived and so far undetermined animal. Modern anthropology, which exploits Nietzsche's writings as eagerly as does psychoanalysis, has completely misunderstood that statement, and totally failed to recognize its implications. Man is the as yet undetermined animal; the rational animal has not yet been brought into its full nature. In order to determine the nature of man so far, man as he has been must first of all be carried beyond himself. Man so far is the last man in that he is not able—and that means, not willing—to subject himself to himself, and to despise what is despicable in his kind as it is so far. This is why a passage beyond himself must be sought for man as he is so far, why the bridge must be found to that nature by which man can overcome his former nature, his last nature. Nietzsche envisaged this nature and kind of self-overcoming man, and at first cast it in the figure of Zarathustra. To this man, who overcomes himself and so subjects himself and so first determines himself, Nietzsche gives a name which is easily misunderstood. He calls him "the superman." But Nietzsche does not mean a type of existing man, only super-dimensional. Nor does he mean a type of man who casts off "humanity," to make sheer caprice the law and titanic rage the rule. The superman is the man who first leads the essential nature of existing man over into its truth, and so assumes that truth. Existing man, by being thus determined and secured in his essential nature, is to be rendered capable of becoming the future master of the earth—of wielding to high purpose the powers that will fall to future man in the nature of the technological transformation of the earth and of human activity. The essential figure of this man, the superman rightly understood, is not a product of an unbridled and degenerate imagination rushing headlong into the void. Nor can it be found by way of an historical analysis of the modern age. No: the superman's essential figure has been presaged to Nietzsche's metaphysical thinking, because his thinking was capable of making a clear junction with the antecedent fate of Western thinking. Nietzsche's thinking gives expression to something that already exists but is still concealed from current views. We may assume, then, that here and there, still invisible to the public eye, the superman already exists. But we must never look for the superman's figure and nature in those characters who by a shallow and misconceived will to power are pushed to the top as the chief functionaries of the various organizations in which that will to power incorporates itself. Nor is the superman a wizard who will lead mankind toward a paradise on earth.

"The wasteland grows; woe to him who hides wastelands within!" Who is he to whom this cry of "woe!" is addressed? He is the superman. For he who passes over must pass away; the superman's way begins with his passing away. By that beginning his way is determined. We must note it once more: because our statement—that the most thought-provoking matter in our thought-provoking time is that we are still not thinking—is connected with Nietzsche's words about the growing wasteland, and because these words, on the other hand, are spoken with the superman in mind, we must try to make the superman's essential nature clear, to the extent to which our own way requires it.

Let us keep clear now of those false, confusing connotations that the word "superman" has to the common understanding. Instead, let us keep our minds on three simple matters that seem to suggest themselves by the word "superman" understood in its plain meaning:

1. The passing over.
2. The site from which the passage leaves.
3. The site to which the passage goes.

The superman goes beyond, overpasses man as he is, the last man. Man, unless he stops with the type of man as he is, is a passage, a transition; he is a bridge; he is "a rope strung between the animal and the superman." The superman, strictly understood, is the figure and form of man to which he who passes over is passing over. Zarathustra himself is not yet the superman, but only the very first to pass over to him—he is the superman in the process of becoming. For various reasons, we limit our reflections here to this preliminary figure of the superman. But we must first give heed to the passage across. Next, we must give closer thought to the second point, the site of departure of him

who crosses over—that is, how matters stand with man as
he is so far, the last man. And third, we must give thought
to where he goes who passes across, that is, what stance
man comes to take as he passes across.

The first point, the passage across, will become clear to
us only as we give thought to the second and third points,
the whence and the whither of the man who passes over and
who, in passing over, is transformed.

The man whom he who passes over overpasses is man as
he is so far. To remind us of that man's essential definition,
Nietzsche calls him the as yet undetermined animal. This
implies: *homo est animal rationale*. "Animal" does not
mean just any living being; plants, too, have life, yet we
cannot call man a rational vegetable. "Animal" means
beast. Man is the beast endowed with reason. Reason is the
perception of what is, which always means also what can be
and ought to be. To perceive implies, in ascending order:
to welcome and take in; to accept and take in the encounter; to take up face to face; to undertake and see through—
and this means to talk through. The Latin for talking
through is *reor*; the Greek ῥέω (as in rhetoric) is the ability
to take up something and see it through; *reri* is *ratio; animal rationale* is the animal which lives by perceiving what
is, in the manner described. The perception that prevails
within reason produces and adduces purposes, establishes
rules, provides means and ways, and attunes reason to the
modes of action. Reason's perception unfolds as this manifold providing, which is first of all and always a confrontation, a face-to-face presentation. Thus one might also say:
homo est animal rationale—man is the animal that confronts face-to-face. A mere animal, such as a dog, never
confronts anything, it can never confront anything *to its
face*; to do so, the animal would have to perceive *itself*. It
cannot say "I," it cannot talk at all. By contrast man,
according to metaphysical doctrine, is the confronting animal which has the property that it can speak. Upon this

essential definition—which is, however, never thought through more fully to its roots—there is then constructed the doctrine of man as the person, which doctrine can thereafter be expressed theologically. *Persona* means the actor's mask through which his dramatic tale is sounded. Since man is the percipient who perceives what is, we can think of him as the *persona*, the mask, of Being.

Nietzsche characterizes the last man as prevailing man in the process, so to speak, of fortifying in himself human nature as it is so far. This is the reason why the last man has only the remotest possibility of passing beyond himself and so keeping himself under his own control. In this species of last man, therefore, reason—the forming of representational ideas—will inevitably perish in a peculiar way and, as it were, become self-ensnarled. Ideas then limit themselves to whatever happens to be provided at the moment—the kind of provisions that are supplied at the enterprise and pleasure of the human manner of forming ideas, and are pleased to be generally comprehensible and palatable. Whatever exists, appears only to the extent to which it is so provided, and only thereby admitted under this tacit planning of ideas, as an object or a state of things. The last man—the final and definitive type of man so far —fixes himself, and generally all that is, by a specific way of representing ideas.

But now we must listen to what Nietzsche himself has Zarathustra say about the last man. Let us just mention a few words of it. They are in the *Prologue*, section 5, of *Thus Spoke Zarathustra* (1883). Zarathustra speaks his prologue in the marketplace of the town to which he came first, having descended from the mountains. The town "lay on the edge of the forest." A large crowd gathered because they had been promised that there would be a tightrope walker, that is, a man who passes across.

One morning, Zarathustra had broken off his ten-year

stay in the mountains to go back down among men. Nietzsche writes:

". . . one morning he rose with the dawn, stepped
before the sun, and spoke to it thus:

" 'You great star, what would your happiness be had
you not those for whom you shine?

" 'For ten years you have climbed to my cave: you
would have tired of your light and of the journey had it
not been for me and my eagle and my serpent.' "

These words—which historically reach back to the heart
of Plato's metaphysics and thus go to the core of Western
thought—conceal the key to Nietzsche's *Thus Spoke Zarathustra*. Zarathustra descended the mountains in solitude.
But when he came into the forest, he there met an old
hermit "who had left his holy cottage." When Zarathustra
was alone again after talking to the old man, he said to his
heart: "Could it be possible? This old saint in the forest has
not yet heard anything of this, that God is dead" (section
2). When he arrives in the marketplace of the town, Zarathustra tries directly to teach the people "the superman" as
"the meaning of the earth." But the people only laughed
at Zarathustra, who had to realize that the time had not yet
come, and that this was not yet the right way, to speak at
once and straight out of the highest and of the future—that
it was advisable to speak only indirectly and even, for the
moment, of the opposite.

"Then I shall speak to them of what is most contempti-
ble; and that is the *last man*." Let us listen only to a few
sentences from this speech about the last man—from this
prologue to what Zarathustra "speaks" in his speeches
proper—to learn what this type of human being is from
which the passage across shall take place.

And thus spoke Zarathustra to the people:
Alas, the time is coming when man will no longer shoot

the arrow of his longing beyond man, and the string of his bow will have forgotten how to whir! . . .

Alas, the time is coming when man will no longer give birth to a star. Alas, the time of the most despicable man is coming, he that is no longer able to despise himself.

Behold, I show you the *last man*. 'What is love? What is creation? What is longing? What is a star?'—thus asks the last man, and he blinks.

The earth has become smaller, and on it hops the last man who makes everything small. His race is as ineradicable as the flea-beetle; the last man lives longest. 'We have invented happiness'—say the last men, and they blink."*

Summary and Transition

We are trying to look in the direction in which Nietzsche's thinking proceeds, because it is the way that gave rise to the words: "The wasteland grows; woe to him who hides wastelands within!" These words in turn are supposed to be clarified by the statement: "Most thought-provoking in our thought-provoking time is that we are still not thinking." The wasteland, the growing of the wasteland—a curiously contradictory turn of phrase! And the hiding of inner wastelands would be connected, then, with the fact that we are still not thinking—connected, that is, with the long since dominant kind of thinking, with the dominance of ideational or representational thinking. The words of our statement, about what is most thought-provoking in our age, would then hark back to Nietzsche's words. Our

* Translation by Walter Kaufmann, from *The Portable Nietzsche*, The Viking Press, New York, copyright 1954.

statement would join with Nietzsche's words in a destiny to which, it seems, our whole earth is destined to its remotest corners. That destiny will above all shake the foundations of all of man's thinking, in dimensions of such magnitude that the demise we moderns are witnessing in only one sector, literature, is a mere episode by comparison. But we must not equate such a shaking of the foundations with revolution and collapse. The shaking of that which exists may be the way by which an equilibrium arises, a position of rest such as has never been—because that rest, that peace, is already present at the heart of the shock.

No thinking, therefore, creates for itself the element in which it operates. But all thinking strives, as if automatically, to stay within the element assigned to it.

What is the element in which Nietzsche's thought operates? We must see more clearly here before attempting further steps along our way. We must see that all those foreground things which Nietzsche had to reject and oppose—that fundamentally he passes them all by, that he speaks only in order better to preserve his silence. He is the first to pose the thoughtful question—thoughtful in that it starts from metaphysics and points back to metaphysics— which we formulate as follows: Is the man of today in his metaphysical nature prepared to assume dominion over the earth as a whole? Has the man of today yet given thought in any way to what conditions will determine the nature of such worldwide government? Is the nature of this man of today such that it is fit to manage those powers, and put to use those means of power, which are released as the nature of modern technology unfolds, forcing man to unfamiliar decisions? Nietzsche's answer to these questions is *No*. Man as he is today is not prepared to form and assume a world government. For today's man lags behind, not just here and there—no, in everything he is, in all his ways, he lags curiously behind that which is and has long been. That

which really is, Being, which from the start calls and determines all beings, can never be made out, however, by
ascertaining facts, by appealing to particulars. That sound
common sense which is so often "cited" in such attempts is
not as sound and natural as it pretends. It is above all not
as absolute as it acts, but rather the shallow product of that
manner of forming ideas which is the final fruit of the
Enlightenment in the eighteenth century. Sound common
sense is always trimmed to fit a certain conception of what
is and ought to be and may be. The power of this curious
understanding extends into our own age; but it is no longer
adequate. The organizations of social life, rearmament in
moral matters, the grease paint of the culture enterprise—
none of them any longer reach what *is*. With all the good
intentions and all the ceaseless effort, these attempts are no
more than makeshift patchwork, expedients for the moment. And why? Because the ideas of aims, purposes, and
means, of effects and causes, from which all those attempts
arise—because these ideas are from the start incapable of
holding themselves open to what is.

There is the danger that the thought of man today will
fall short of the decisions that are coming, decisions of
whose specific historical shape we can know nothing—that
the man of today will look for these decisions where they
can never be made.

What did the Second World War really decide? (We
shall not mention here its fearful consequences for my
country, cut in two.) This world war has decided nothing
—if we here use "decision" in so high and wide a sense
that it concerns solely man's essential fate on this earth.
Only the things that have remained undecided stand out
somewhat more clearly. But even here, the danger is growing again that those matters in this undecided area which
are moving toward a decision, and which concern world
government as a whole—that these matters, which now

must be decided, will once again be forced into politico-social and moral categories that are in all respects too narrow and faint-hearted, and thus will be deprived of a possible befitting consideration and reflection.

Even in the decade from 1920 to 1930, the European world of ideas could not cope any longer with what was then looming on the horizon. What is to become of a Europe that wants to rebuild itself with the stage props of those years after World War I? A plaything for the powers, and for the immense native strength of the Eastern peoples. In his *Twilight of the Idols, or, How to Philosophize with a Hammer*, written in the summer of 1888, Nietzsche writes, in the section "Critique of Modernity": "Our institutions are good for nothing any more: on this point all agree. However, it is not their fault but *ours*. Now that we have mislaid all the instincts from which institutions grow, we lose institutions altogether because *we* are no longer good for them. Democracy has always been the form of decline in organizing power: in *Human, All Too Human* I, 349 (1878) I already characterized modern democracy, together with its mongrel forms such as the 'German Reich,' as the *form of decline of the state*. If there are to be institutions there must be a kind of will, instinct, imperative, anti-liberal to the point of malice: the will to tradition, to authority, to responsibility for centuries to come, to the *solidarity* of chains of generations forward and backward *ad infinitum*. When that will is present, something like the *Imperium Romanum* is founded: or something like Russia, the *only* power today that has endurance in its bones, that can wait, that still can have promise—Russia the counter-concept to that miserable European particularism and nervousness which has entered a critical condition with the foundation of the German Reich. . . . The whole West no longer possesses those instincts out of which institutions grow, out of which a *future* grows: nothing else, perhaps, goes so much against the grain of its 'modern spirit.' Men live for the day, men live very fast—men live very irresponsibly: precisely this is called 'freedom.' The thing that *makes* an institution an institution is despised, hated, rejected: men fear they are in danger of a new slavery the moment the word 'authority' is even mentioned." (W.W., VIII, p. 150 f.).

In order to forestall any misinterpretation on the part of sound common sense, let it be noted that the "Russia" Nietzsche has in mind is not identical with today's political and economic system of the Soviet republics. Nietzsche's concern is to think beyond the teeming multitude of nationalisms which, as he saw even then, are no longer viable, and to clear the field for the great decisions—for reflection upon these decisions. The reason why man is lagging behind that which is, Nietzsche sees in the fact that prevailing human nature is still not fully developed and secured. According to an ancient doctrine of metaphysics, man is the rational animal. This conception, which goes back to the Romans, no longer answers to what the Greeks had in mind with the name $\zeta\tilde{\omega}o\nu$ $\lambda\acute{o}\gamma o\nu$ $\check{\epsilon}\chi o\nu$. According to that doctrine, man is "that rising presence which can make appear what is present." In the world of Western conceptions and ideas that was to follow, man becomes a peculiarly constructed combination of animality and rationality. But to Nietzsche, neither the nature of animality, nor the nature of reason, nor the proper essential unity of the two, is as yet determined, that is, established and secured. Therefore, the two domains of being, animality and rationality, separate and clash. This rupture prevents man from possessing unity of nature and thus being free for what we normally call the real. Therefore, it is a most important part of Nietzsche's way of thought to go beyond man as he is so far, beyond man in his as yet undetermined nature, into the complete determination of his whole nature up to this point. Fundamentally, Nietzsche's way of thought does not want to overthrow anything—it merely wants to catch up to something. To the passage beyond man as he is so far, Nietzsche gives the much misunderstood and much abused name "superman." Let me stress it again: the superman in Nietzsche's sense is not man as he exists until now, only superdimensional. The "superman" does not simply carry the accustomed drives and strivings of the customary type of man beyond all measure and bounds. Superman is qualitatively, not quantitatively, different from existing man. The thing that the superman discards is precisely our boundless, purely quantitative nonstop progress. The superman is poorer, simpler, tenderer and tougher, quieter and more self-sacrificing and slower of decision, and more economical of speech. Nor does the superman appear in droves, or at random—he appears only after the rank order has been carried out. By rank order in its essential meaning —not merely in the sense of an arrangement of existing conditions according to this or that scale—Nietzsche understands the standard that all men are not equal, that not everybody has aptitude and claim to everything, that not everybody may set up his everyman's tribunal to judge everything. In a note to his *Zarathustra* (which he himself did not publish, however) Nietzsche writes: "The rank order carried out, in a system of world government: the masters of the earth last of all, a new ruling caste. Arising from them, here and there, all Epicurean god, the superman, he who transfigures existence: *Caesar with the soul of Christ.*"

We must not pass over these words in too great a hurry— especially since they bring to mind other words, spoken even more deeply and more secretly, in one of Hoelderlin's late hymns: there Christ, who is "of still another nature," is called the brother of Heracles and Dionysos—so that there is announced here a still unspoken gathering of the whole of Western fate, the gathering from which alone the Occident can go forth to meet the coming decisions— to become, perhaps and in a wholly other mode, a land of dawn, an Orient.

The superman constitutes a transformation and thus a rejection of man so far. Accordingly, the public figures who in the course of current history emerge in the limelight are as far from the superman's nature as is humanly possible.

In the course of these lectures, we can offer no more than a sketchy outline of the superman's essential nature, and even this only for the primary purpose of preventing the crudest misunderstandings and mistaken attitudes concerning Nietzsche's thought—and in order to show some points of view from which we may prepare to take the first steps toward a *confrontation* with Nietzsche's thought.

The thinking of today—if we may call it that—lacks nearly every qualification needed to interpret the figure of Nietzsche's Zarathustra, let alone confront Nietzsche's basic metaphysical doctrines; these two tasks are at bottom one. Therefore, the first approach to Nietzsche's writings, which may easily remain decisive for the future, encounters almost insuperable difficulties if it is made without preparation. Especially when reading *Thus Spoke Zarathustra*, we are only too ready to take and judge what we read by those ideas which we ourselves have brought along unnoticed. This danger is still especially acute for us, because Nietzsche's writings and their publication are very close to us in time, and especially because their language has shaped today's usage more strongly than we know. Still—the closer in time, the more nearly our contemporary a thinker is, the longer is the way to what he has thought, and the less may we shun this long way. This, too, we must still learn, to read a book such as Nietzsche's *Thus Spoke Zarathustra* in the same rigorous manner as one of Aristotle's treatises; the same manner, be it noted, not the identical manner.

For there is no universal schema which could be applied mechanically to the interpretation of the writings of thinkers, or even to a single work of a single thinker. A dialogue of Plato—the *Phaedrus,* for example, the conversation on Beauty—can be interpreted in totally different spheres and respects, according to totally different implications and problematics. This multiplicity of possible interpretations does not discredit the strictness of the thought content. For all true thought remains open to more than one interpretation—and this by reason of its nature. Nor is this multiplicity of possible interpretations merely the residue of a still unachieved formal-logical univocity which we properly ought to strive for but did not attain. Rather, multiplicity of meanings is the element in which all thought must move in order to be strict thought. To use an image: to a fish, the depths and expanses of its waters, the currents and quiet pools, warm and cold layers are the element of its multiple mobility. If the fish is deprived of the fullness of its element, if it is dragged on the dry sand, then it can only wriggle, twitch, and die. Therefore, we always must seek out thinking, and its burden of thought, in the element of its multiple meanings, else everything will remain closed to us.

If we take up one of Plato's dialogues, and scrutinize and judge its "content" in keeping with the ways in which sound common sense forms its ideas—something that happens all too often and too easily—we arrive at the most curious views, and finally at the conviction that Plato must have been a great muddlehead; because we find—and this is indeed correct—that not a single one of Plato's dialogues arrives at a palpable, unequivocal result which sound common sense could, as the saying goes, hold on to. As if sound common sense—the last resort of those who are by nature envious of thinking—as if this common sense whose soundness lies in its immunity to any problematic, had ever

caught on to anything at the source, had ever thought
through anything from its source!

A dialogue of Plato is inexhaustible—not only for posterity and the changing forms of comprehension to which
posterity gives rise; it is inexhaustible of itself, by its nature. And this is forever the mark of all creativeness—
which, of course, comes only to those who are capable of
reverence.

As we apply these thoughts to Nietzsche, we may surmise
that the manner in which the last man forms his ideas is
least fit ever to think freely through what Nietzsche has in
mind with the name "superman."

The superman is first of all a man who goes beyond,
who passes over; hence something of his essential nature is
most likely to become discernible if we follow for a moment
the two aspects that make up his passage.

Where does the crossing-over come from, and where does
it go?

The superman goes beyond man such as he is till now,
and thus goes away from him. What kind of man is he
whom the superman leaves behind? Nietzsche describes
man so far as the last man. "The last man" is the type of
man that immediately precedes the appearance of the superman. The last man, therefore, can be seen for what he is
only with reference to the superman, and only after the
superman's appearance. But we shall never find the superman as long as we look for him in the places of remote-con-
trolled public opinion and on the stock exchanges of the
culture business—all those places where the last man, and
none but he, controls the operation. The superman never
appears in the noisy parades of alleged men of power, nor
in the well-staged meetings of politicians. The superman's
appearance is likewise inaccessible to the teletypers and
radio dispatches of the press which present—that is, represent—events to the public even before they have happened.
This well made-up and well staged manner of forming

ideas, of representation, with its constantly more refined mechanism, dissimulates and blocks from view what really *is*. And this dissimulation and blocking is not just incidental, but is done on the principle of a way of forming ideas whose rule is all-pervading. This type of dissimulating ideas is always supported by sound common sense. The Johnny on the spot, in every area including the literature industry, is the famous "man in the street," always available in the required quantities. Faced with this dissimulating type of representational ideas, thinking finds itself in a contradictory position. This Nietzsche saw clearly. On the one hand, the common ideas and views must be shouted at when they want to set themselves up as the judges of thought, so that men will wake up. On the other hand, thinking can never tell its thoughts by shouting. Next to the words of Nietzsche quoted earlier, about ear-smashing and drum clatter, we must then set those others which run : "It is the stillest words that bring on the storm. Thoughts that come on doves' feet guide the world." (*Thus Spoke Zarathustra*, Part II, "The stillest hour").

Indeed, Nietzsche never did publish what he really thought after *Zarathustra*—something we tend to overlook. All his writings after *Zarathustra* are polemics; they are outcries. What he really thought became known only through the largely inadequate posthumous publications.

From all that has here been suggested, it should be clear that one cannot read Nietzsche in a haphazard way; that each one of his writings has its own character and limits; and that the most important works and labors of his thought, which are contained in his posthumous writings, make demands to which we are not equal. It is advisable, therefore, that you postpone reading Nietzsche for the time being, and first study Aristotle for ten to fifteen years.

How does Nietzsche describe the man whom he who passes over overpasses? Zarathustra says in his prologue: "Behold! I show you the last man."

LECTURE
VII

Listen closely: "The last man lives longest." What does that say? It says that under the last man's dominion, which has now begun, we are by no means approaching an end, a final age, but that the last man will on the contrary have a strangely long staying-power. And on what grounds? Obviously on the grounds of his type of nature, which also determines the way and the "how" in which everything *is*, and in which everything is taken to be.

For the *animal rationale*, this type of nature consists in the way he sets up everything that is, as his objects and subjective states, confronts them, and adjusts to these objects and states as his environing circumstances. What sort of ideas are they with which the last man is concerned? Nietzsche says it clearly, but he does not discuss further what he says in the way in which we now raise the question. What type of idea-forming is it in which the last men linger? The last men blink. What does that mean? *Blink* is related to Middle English *blenchen*, which means deceive, and to *blenken, blinken*, which means gleam or glitter. To blink——that means to play up and set up a glittering deception which is then agreed upon as true and valid——with the mutual tacit understanding not to question the setup. Blinking: the mutual setup, agreed upon and in the end no longer in need of explicit agreement, of the objective and static surfaces and foreground facets of all things as alone valid and valuable—a setup with whose help man carries on and degrades everything.

Summary and Transition

To find what Nietzsche really thought is as difficult as it is to lose it. The difficulty cannot be removed in a few hours of lectures. But it can be pointed out. In fact, a pointer is needed, if only for the reason that we men of today hardly know what it takes to gain access to a thinker, especially one so close to us in time as Nietzsche. The following reflections, however, concern the way of access to the tradition of thinking generally. The best and basically only manner to find out is to go that way. But it takes the devotion of almost a life time. The thinkers' thought is laid down in books. Books are books. The only allowance we make for books in philosophy is that they may be difficult to read. But one book is not like another, especially not when we are concerned with reading a "Book for Everyone and No One." And that is here our concern. For we cannot get around the necessity of finding Nietzsche first, in order that we may then lose him in the sense defined earlier. Why? Because Nietzsche's thinking gives voice and language to what now *is*—but in a language in which the two-thousand-year-old tradition of Western metaphysics speaks, a language which we all speak, which Europe speaks—though in a form transposed more than once, timeworn, shallowed, threadbare, and rootless. Plato and Aristotle speak in what is still our language of today. Parmenides and Heraclitus, too, think in what is still our realm of ideas. But an appeal is made to modern man's historical awareness in order to make us believe that those men are museum pieces of intellectual history, which can occasionally be placed back on exhibit by a display of scholarship. And since we hardly know on what the nature of language rests, we naturally take the view that our motorcycle, for example, standing on the parking lot behind the university, is more real than a thought of Plato about ἰδέα, or Aristotle about ἐνέργεια: thoughts which speak to us still to-day in every scientific concept—and not only there—and make their claim on us, though we pay no attention to this relation, hardly give it a thought.

People still hold the view that what is handed down to us by tradition is what in reality lies behind us—while in fact it comes toward us because we are its captives and destined to it. The purely historical view of tradition and the course of history is one of those vast self-deceptions in which we must remain entangled as long as we are still not really thinking. That self-deception about history prevents us from hearing the language of the thinkers. We do not hear it rightly, because we take that language to be mere expression, setting forth philosophers' views. But the thinkers' language tells what is. To hear it is in no case easy. Hearing it presupposes that we meet a certain requirement, and we do so only on rare occasions. We must acknowledge and respect it. To acknowledge and respect consists in letting every thinker's thought come to us as something in each case unique, never to be repeated, inexhaustible—and being shaken to the depths by what is unthought in his thought. What is unthought in a thinker's thought is not a lack inherent in his thought. What is un-thought is there in each case only as the un-*thought*. The more original the thinking, the richer will be what is unthought in it. The unthought is the greatest gift that thinking can bestow. But to the commonplaces of sound common sense, what is unthought in any thinking always remains merely the incomprehensible. And to the common comprehension, the incomprehensible is never an occasion to stop and look at its own powers of comprehension, still less to notice their limitations. To the common comprehension, what is incomprehensible remains forever merely offensive—proof enough to such comprehension, which is convinced it was born comprehending everything, that it is now being imposed upon with an untruth and sham. The one thing of which sound common sense is least capable is acknowledgment and respect. For acknowledgment and respect call for a readiness to let our own attempts at thinking be overturned, again and again, by what is unthought in the thinkers' thought. Someone who knew better, Kant, here spoke of a "falling down." But no one can fall down who does not stand upright, and standing upright walks, and walking stays upon the way. The way leads necessarily into face-to-face converse with the thinkers. It is not necessary here, however, to conceive of this converse historically. For instance, if we were to give out grades by the standards of the history of philosophy, Kant's historical comprehension of Aristotle and Plato would have to get a straight "F." Yet Kant and only Kant has creatively transformed Plato's doctrine of ideas.

One thing is necessary, though, for a face-to-face converse with the thinkers: clarity about the manner in which we encounter them. Basically, there are only two possibilities: either to go to their encounter, or to go counter to them. If we want to go to the encounter of a thinker's thought, we must magnify still further what is great in him. Then we will enter into what is unthought in his thought. If we wish only to go counter to a thinker's thought, this wish must have minimized beforehand what is great in him. We then shift his thought into the commonplaces of our know-it-all presumption. It makes no difference if we assert in passing that Kant was nonetheless a very significant thinker. Such praises from below are always an insult.

We could leave sound common sense to its own devices if its obstinacy did not again and again crop up *within ourselves,* even when we make every effort to abandon the commonplace, the obvious as the standard of thinking. We could ignore the stubbornness of sound common sense, if only it would not spread itself so, particularly in the case of Nietzsche. For notwithstanding many exaggerations and dark allusions, everything Nietzsche offers to our thought looks largely as if it were perfectly obvious—including even the book *Thus Spoke Zarathustra,* including even his doctrine of the superman. But that is pure illusion. The doctrine of the superman, which by its nature can never be an anthropology, belongs, like every metaphysical doctrine of man, among the basic doctrines of every metaphysics; it belongs to the doctrine of the Being of beings. One might ask, then, why we do not at once present Nietzsche's doctrine of the superman in the light of his basic metaphysical doctrine of Being. We do not, for two reasons: first, Nietzsche himself presents his basic metaphysical doctrine, his doctrine of the Being of beings, through the doctrine of the superman, in keeping with the unequivocal trend of all modern metaphysics; and second, we of today, despite our interest in metaphysics and ontology, are scarcely able any longer properly to raise even the *question* of the Being of beings—to raise it in a way which will put in question our own being so that it becomes questionable in its relatedness to Being, and thereby open to Being.

It now becomes possible to answer a question raised repeatedly about this lecture series. When we hazarded here a reference to Nietzsche's thought, and chose his doctrine of the superman, we did not at all propose an attempt to reinterpret, transform and dissolve Nietzsche's metaphysics into a doctrine of human nature, into an "existential anthropology"—as though Nietzsche had inquired only about man, and merely on occasion and incidentally touched on the question of the Being of beings. Conversely, a presentation of Nietzsche's doctrine of the Being of beings could never undertake to treat his doctrine of the superman as merely incidental, still less push it aside as a position he presumably abandoned.

Every philosophical—that is, thoughtful—doctrine of man's essential nature is *in itself alone* a doctrine of the Being of beings. Every doctrine of Being is *in itself alone* a doctrine of man's essential nature. But neither doctrine can be obtained by merely turning the other one around. Why this is so, and generally the question of this relation existing between man's nature and the Being of beings— this is in fact the one single question which all traditional thinking must first be brought to face; a question which was still unknown even to Nietzsche. But it is a question of abysmal difficulty, simply because our seemingly correct posing of the question in fact muddles the question fundamentally. We ask what the relation is between man's nature and the Being of beings. But—as soon as I thoughtfully say "man's nature," I have already said relatedness to Being. Likewise, as soon as I say thoughtfully: Being of beings, the relatedness to man's nature has been named. Each of the two members of the relation between man's nature and Being already implies the relation itself. To speak to the heart of the matter: there is no such thing here as members of the relation, nor the relation as such. Accordingly, the situation we have named between man's nature and the Being of beings allows no dialectical maneuvers in which one member of the relation is played off against the other. This state of affairs—not only that all dialectic fails in this case, but that there is simply no place left for a failure of this kind—is probably what is most offensive to today's habits of idea-forming and most unsettling to the skilled acrobats of its empty astuteness.

No way of thought, not even the way of metaphysical

thought, begins with man's essential nature and goes on from there to Being, nor in reverse from Being and then back to man. Rather, every way of thinking *takes its way* already *within* the total relation of Being and man's nature, or else it is not thinking at all. The oldest axioms of Western thought, of which we shall hear more, already state this fact. This is why Nietzsche's way, too, is so marked almost from the start. To show it quickly and unmistakably, rather than by long-winded explications, I quote the first and the last sentence from the "autobiography" which the nineteen-year-old Nietzsche wrote in his student days at Schulpforta. Schulpforta, near Naumburg on the river Saale, was one of the most famous and influential schools of nineteenth-century Germany. The manuscript of this autobiography was found in 1935, in a chest in the attic of the Nietzsche Archives in Weimar. In 1936 it was published in a facsimile brochure, as a model for the young. That brochure has long since gone out of print and is forgotten. The first sentence in his description of his life up to that time reads:

"I was born as a plant near the churchyard, as a man in a pastor's house."

The last sentence reads:

"Thus man grows out of everything that once embraced him; he has no need to break the shackles—they fall away unforeseen, when a god bids them; and where is the ring that in the end still encircles him? Is it the world? Is it God?"

Even the later Nietzsche, the man who, in the last year of his creativity and after losing balance more than once, wrote the terrible book *The Antichrist*, was still asking the same question—if only we can and will read it. However—to hear this questioning, to come close to his ways of thought, one requires here to respect and to acknowledge. Respecting and acknowledging are not yet agreement; but it is the necessary precondition for any confrontation. Nietzsche's way is marked with the name "the superman."

LECTURE VIII

The superman is the man who passes over, away from man as he is so far, but away whereto? Man so far is the last man. But if this manner of living being, "man," in distinction from other living beings on earth, plants and animals, is endowed with "rationality"; and if *ratio*, the power to perceive and reckon with things, is at bottom a way of forming ideas; then the particular manner of the last man must consist in a particular manner of forming ideas. Nietzsche calls it blinking, without relating blinking explicitly to the nature of representing or idea-forming, without inquiring into the essential sphere, and above all the essential origin, of representational ideas. But we must nonetheless give its full weight to the term Nietzsche uses for this kind of ideation, namely, blinking, according to the context in which it appears. We must not take it to be the same thing as the merely superficial and incidental wink by which we signal to each other on special occasions that in fact we are no longer taking seriously what is being said and proposed, and what goes on in general. This kind of winking can spread only because all forming of ideas is itself a kind of blinking. Ideas formed in this way present and propose of everything only the glitter, only the appearance of surfaces and foreground facets. Only what is so proposed and so disposed has currency. This type of representation is not first created by blinking, but the other way around: the blinking is a consequence of a type of representation already dominant. What type? The type that constitutes the metaphysical basis of the age called the Modern Age, which is not ending now but only just beginning, since the Being that prevails in it is only now unfolding into the predestined totality of beings. This metaphysical basis of the modern age cannot be explained in a few sentences. I refer you to a lecture I gave here in 1938, published in my book *Timber Tracks* under the title "The Time of the World View."

"We have invented happiness, say the last men, and blink."

We shall see to it from every angle, with the aid of our sociology, psychology and psychotherapy, and by some other means besides, that all men are soon placed in identical conditions of identical happiness in the identical way, and that the identity of the welfare of all men is secured. Yet, despite this invention of happiness, man is driven from one world war into the next. With a wink the nations are informed that peace is the elimination of war, but that meanwhile this peace which eliminates war can be secured only by war. Against this war-peace, in turn, we launch a peace offensive whose attacks can hardly be called peaceful. War—the securing of peace; and peace—the elimination of war. How is peace to be secured by what it eliminates? Something is fundamentally out of joint here, or perhaps it has never yet been in joint. Meanwhile, "war" and "peace" are still like the two sticks that savages rub together to make fire. Meanwhile, the last man must move in a realm of ideas which blink at everything and can do nothing else but blink, in consequence of an unearthly fate that forbids modern man to look beyond himself and his type of ideas. He has no other choice but to search among his type of ideas—blinking—for the form of those measures that are to create a world order. The congresses and conferences, committees and sub-committees—are they anything other than the blinking organizations of blinking arrangements of distrust and treachery? Any decision in this realm of ideas must by its very nature fall short. Even so, man cannot settle down, in indecision, to a sham peace and security. Still, the source of man's inner fragmentation remains shrouded in the shadows of an unearthly world destiny. That shroud itself is further covered up by the predominance of publicity, so that the fracture of his fragmentation does not yet reach down to man in his essence, despite all the unspeakable suffering, all the distress that all too many men endure. The pain that rises from the rift of that which is, does not yet reach man in his essence. What did we say at the end of the first lecture? "We feel no pain. . . ."

After all that has been said, could it be that this blinking way of forming ideas lies beyond the reach of man's mere whims, even his carelessness? Could it be that there prevails in that realm a peculiar relation regarding that which is, a relation that reaches beyond man? Could this relation be of such a kind that it will not allow man to let Being in its essence be?

Could it be that this way of forming ideas does indeed face what is, does indeed face beings, and yet at bottom opposes everything that is and as it is? Could it be that this manner of forming ideas at bottom sets upon everything it sets before itself, in order to depose and decompose it? What manner of thinking is it that sets all things up in such a way that fundamentally it pursues and sets upon them? What is the spirit of this manner of representation? What type of thinking is it that in thought pursues everything in this manner? Of what kind is the pursuit of thought by man so far?

Nietzsche gives us an answer concerning that way of forming ideas which prevails from the start and pervades all of the last man's blinking. It is in the third section from the end of Part Two of *Thus Spoke Zarathustra* (1883), entitled "On Deliverance." There it says:

> "*The spirit of revenge*, my friends, has so far been the subject of man's best reflection; and wherever there was suffering, there punishment was also wanted."

To "*wreak* revenge," the Middle English *wreken*, the German *Rache*, the Latin *urgere*—all signify "to press close and hard," "drive," "drive out," "banish," "pursue." The pursuit of thought, the formation of ideas of man so far is determined by revenge, the onset, the attack. But if Nietzsche wants to get away from man so far and his form of ideas, and go on to another and higher man, what then will be the bridge which leads to the way passing across? In what direction does Nietzsche's thought point when he seeks that bridge to get away from the last man, and across to the superman? What was this thinker's true and one and only thought, which he thought even if he did not announce it on every occasion or always in the same way? Nietzsche gives the answer in the same Part Two of *Thus Spoke Zarathustra*, in the section "On the Tarantulas":

> "For *that man be delivered from revenge:* that is the bridge to the highest hope for me, and a rainbow after long storms."

Summary and Transition

We ask: What is called thinking?—and we talk about Nietzsche. This observation is correct, and yet in error because it blinds us to what is being said. Hence, what is being talked about and what is being said are not identical. We may have a correct idea of what is being talked about, and yet may not have let ourselves become involved in what is being said. What is being said is what Nietzsche is thinking. As a thinker, he thinks what is, in what respect it is, and in what way it is. He thinks that which is, particular beings in their Being. The thinkers' thinking would thus be the relatedness to the Being of beings. If we follow what the thinker Nietzsche thinks, we operate within this relatedness to Being. We are thinking. To say it more circumspectly, we are attempting to let ourselves become involved in this relatedness to Being. We are attempting to learn thinking.

We are talking about Nietzsche, but we are asking: what is it that is called thinking, what does call for thinking? But we pursue only what Nietzsche says about the superman. Even then we are inquiring about the superman's nature only to the extent to which he is the man who passes over. We are intent on the passage across. From this point of view, we ask what he goes away from, and where he goes who goes across. Thus we are asking about the bridge for the passage across. But we are by no means asking about the Being of beings. What is more, our question about the bridge for the passage across has brought us up against a peculiar and singular thing. What, for Nietzsche, is the bridge to the highest hope—to the essential form of man who goes beyond man so far? That bridge is for him "the deliverance from revenge." According to Nietzsche, the spirit of revenge marks man as he is so far, and most completely the last man. However, the overcoming of vengefulness is patently a separate problem which concerns moral conduct, the morality of man's behavior and attitude. The discussion of vengefulness and its overcoming belongs to the field of ethics and morals. How then are we, who are pursuing this separate question of revenge and its overcoming, how are we supposed to be dealing with Nietzsche's thought proper, that is, with the relatedness to Being? The

question of revenge and its overcoming is no doubt important, but still it is quite remote from the question of what
is. The question of revenge is after all not the question of
Being. Let us see. Let us learn thinking.

LECTURE
IX

———◆———

Nietzsche's thinking focuses on deliverance from the spirit of revenge. It focuses on a spirit which, being the freedom from revenge, is prior to all mere fraternization, but also to any mere desire to mete out punishment, to all peace efforts and all warmongering—prior to that other spirit which would establish and secure peace, *pax*, by pacts. The space of this freedom from revenge is prior to all pacifism, and equally to all power politics. It is prior to all weak do-nothingism and shirking of sacrifice, and to blind activity for its own sake. The space of freedom from revenge is where Nietzsche sees the superman's essential nature. That is the space toward which he who crosses over is moving— the superman—"Caesar with the *soul* of Christ."

Nietzsche's thinking focuses on the spirit of freedom from revenge—this is his alleged free-thinking. If we will just keep this basic trait of his thought in mind however vaguely, the prevailing image of Nietzsche—which is already deeply rooted in the current views—is bound to crumble.

We are trying to mark out the way of him who crosses over, that is, the passage and transition from the last man to the superman. We are asking for the bridge from the one to the other. The bridge, in Nietzsche's own words, is the deliverance from revenge.

As has already been suggested, one could take the view that the problem of revenge, and of deliverance from revenge, is peculiar to ethics and moral education—while the anatomy of the desire for revenge, as a basic trait of man and thought so far, is a task for "psychology." Judged by their wording, and even by their headings, Nietzsche's discussions do indeed move in the traditional conceptual framework of ethics and psychology. But in substance, Nietzsche thinks of everything that falls under the heads of "ethics" and "psychology" in terms of metaphysics, that is, with a view to the question how the Being of beings as a whole is determined, and how it concerns man. "Ethics" and "psychology" are grounded in metaphysics. When it comes to saving man's essential nature, psychology—whether as such or in the form of psychotherapy—is helpless; ethics as a mere doctrine and imperative is helpless unless man first comes to have a different fundamental relation to Being—unless man of his own accord, so far as in him lies, begins at last to hold his nature open for once to the essential relation toward Being, no matter whether Being specifically addresses itself to man, or whether it still lets him be speechless because he is painless. But even if we do no more than bear and endure this speechlessness and painlessness, our nature is already open to the claim of Being. Yet even this openness to Being, which thinking can prepare, is of itself helpless to save man. A real openness in his relatedness to Being is a necessary though not sufficient condition for saving him. And yet, precisely when thinking plies its proper trade, which is to rip away the fog that conceals beings as such, it must be concerned not to cover up the rift. Hegel once expressed the point as follows, though only in a purely metaphysical respect and dimension: "Better a mended sock than a torn one—not so with self-consciousness." Sound common sense, bent on utility, sides with the "mended" sock. On the other hand, reflection on the sphere in which particular beings are revealed—

which is for modern philosophy the sphere of subjectivity—
is on the side of the torn condition—the torn consciousness.
Through the rift, torn consciousness is open to admit the
Absolute. This holds true for thinking: . . . The torn
condition keeps the way open into metaphysics.

And metaphysics in its widest meaning—in fact the very
core of metaphysics—is the sphere where we must from the
start place Nietzsche's thinking on revenge, and on deliverance from revenge. Our remarks here must necessarily
remain very general, and must keep constant touch with
the words about the growing wasteland.

Still, any such remarks will take us step by step, sentence
by sentence, into a difficult landscape which is remote, however, from the almost airless spaces of dead concepts and
luxuriant abstractions. This landscape is in a land on whose
grounds all movements of our modern age take place. The
fact that we do not see or rather do not want to see these
grounds, much less this land, is no proof that they are not
there.

In order to understand that—and how—Nietzsche from
the very start thinks of revenge and the deliverance from revenge in metaphysical terms, that is, in the light of Being
which determines all particular beings, we must note in
what form the nature of the Being of beings makes its
appearance in the modern era. The form of the nature of
Being which we have in mind has found its classic formulation in a few sentences which Schelling wrote in 1809, in
his *Philosophical Investigation Concerning the Nature of
Human Freedom and its Object*. The three sentences that
follow are expressly set off in Schelling's text by a hyphen
from what went before, further emphasizing their fundamental importance. They run:

"In the final and highest instance, there is no being
other than willing. Willing is primal being and to it
alone [willing] belong all [primal being's] predicates:

being unconditioned, eternity, independence of time, self-affirmation. All philosophy strives only to find this highest expression" (Works, Section I, vol. 7, p. 350).

The predicates, then, which metaphysical thought has since antiquity attributed to Being, Schelling finds in their final, highest and hence most perfected form in willing. The will in this willing does not mean here a capacity of the human soul, however; the word "willing" here designates the Being of beings as a whole. Every single being and all beings as a whole have their essential powers in and through the will. That sounds strange to us; and it will remain strange as long as we remain strangers to the essential and simple thoughts of occidental metaphysics, in other words, as long as we do not think those thoughts but merely go on forever reporting them. It is possible, for example, to ascertain historically down to the last detail what Leibniz said about the Being of beings, and yet not to understand in the least what Leibniz thought when he defined the Being of beings from the perspective of the monad, and defined the monad as the unity of *perceptio* and *appetitus*, as the oneness of perception and appetite. What Leibniz thought is then expressed by Kant and Fichte as the rational will, which Hegel and Schelling, each in his own way, reflect upon. Schopenhauer names and intends the same thing when he thinks of the world as will and idea; and Nietzsche thinks the same thing when he defines the primal nature of beings as the will to power. That the Being of beings appears here invariably and always as will, is not because a few philosophers have formed opinions about Being. What this appearance of Being as will points to is something that cannot be found out by any amount of scholarship. Only the inquiry of thought can approach it, only thought can do justice to its problematic, only thought can keep it thoughtfully in mind and memory.

To modern metaphysics, the Being of beings appears as

will. But inasmuch as man, because of his nature as the thinking animal and by virtue of forming ideas, is related to beings in their Being, is thereby related to Being, and is thus determined by Being—therefore man's being, in keeping with this relatedness of Being (which now means, of the will) to human nature, must emphatically appear as a willing.

How, then, does Nietzsche think of the nature of revenge if he thinks of it metaphysically? We may explain the question with this other question: what is the nature of revenge, if its pursuit determines all ideas? The idea sets before us that which is. It determines and sets down what may pass as having being. The determination of what is, then, is in a certain way at the command of a way of forming ideas which pursues and sets upon everything in order to set it up and maintain it in its own way.

Since long ago, that which is present has been regarded as what is. But what representational ideas can we form of what in a way is no longer, and yet still is? What ideas can we form of that which was? At this "it was," idea and its willing take offense. Faced with what "was," willing no longer has anything to say. Faced with every "it was," willing no longer has anything to propose. This "it was" resists the willing of that will. The "it was" becomes a stumbling block for all willing. It is the block which the will can no longer budge. Then the "it was" becomes the sorrow and despair of all willing which, being what it is, always wills forward, and is always foiled by the bygones that lie fixed firmly in the past. Thus the "it was" is revolting and contrary to the will. This is why revulsion against the "it was" arises in the will itself when it is faced with this contrary "it was." But by way of this revulsion, the contrary takes root within willing itself. Willing endures the contrary within itself as a heavy burden; it suffers from it—that is, the will suffers from itself. Willing appears to itself as this

suffering from the "it was," as the suffering from the by-
gone, the past. But what is past stems from the passing. The
will—in suffering from this passing, yet being what it is
precisely by virtue of this suffering—remains in its willing
captive to the passing. Thus will itself wills passing. It wills
the passing of its suffering, and thus wills its own passing.
The will's revulsion against every "it was" appears as the
will to pass away, which wills that everything be worthy of
passing away. The revulsion arising in the will is then the
will against everything that passes—everything, that is,
which comes to be out of a coming-to-be, and endures.
Hence the will is the sphere of representational ideas which
basically pursue and set upon everything that comes and
goes and exists, in order to depose, reduce it in its stature
and ultimately decompose it. This revulsion within the will
itself, according to Nietzsche, is the essential nature of
revenge.

> "This, yes, this alone is *revenge* itself: the will's re-
> vulsion against time and its 'It was'." (*Thus Spoke
> Zarathustra*, Part II, "On Deliverance.")

Revenge, however, never calls itself by its own name,
least of all when it is in the act of taking revenge. Revenge
calls itself "punishment." By this name it endows its hostile
nature with the semblance of right and justice. It covers
its revolting nature with the semblance that it is meting
out well-deserved punishment.

> " 'Punishment'—that is what revenge calls itself:
> with a lying word it counterfeits a good conscience"
> (*ibid.*) .

This is not the place to discuss whether these words of
Nietzsche, on revenge and punishment, revenge and suffering, revenge and deliverance from revenge, represent a
direct confrontation with Schopenhauer, and indirectly one

with all world-denying attitudes. We must turn our attention elsewhere to see the full implications of his thoughts about revenge, and to understand where Nietzsche is really looking for deliverance from revenge. Then we shall be able to see within what limits Nietzsche's thinking about revenge is moving. In that way, the realm of his thinking as a whole will emerge more distinctly. Then it is bound to become clear in what way Nietzsche, while speaking of revenge, thinks about the Being of beings as a whole. It is bound to become clear that Nietzsche does in fact think of nothing else than the Being of beings when he thinks of the spirit of revenge and of deliverance from revenge. And if all this is so, then Nietzsche's question about revenge, rightly thought through, will lead us to the fundamental position of his thought, that is, into the heart and core of his metaphysics. Once we reach that heartland, we are in the realm from which the words were spoken: "The wasteland grows . . ." Now, if the spirit of revenge determines all thinking so far, and this thinking is essentially a forming of ideas, then a long perspective is bound to open up on the nature and essence of representational ideas. We shall have an open view of the area in which thinking so far is moving—even Nietzsche's own thinking.

In order to see how far Nietzsche's thought about revenge carries metaphysically, or rather how far it is carried, we must note how he sees and defines the nature of revenge. Nietzsche says:

"This, yes, this alone is *revenge* itself: the will's revulsion against time and its 'It was'."

That a description of revenge should stress what is revolting and refractory in revenge, and thus runs counter to the will, seems to be in the nature of the case. But Nietzsche's thought goes further. He does not say simply: Revenge is revulsion—just as we might describe hatred as refractory and detracting. Nietzsche says : Revenge is the will's revulsion. We have since noted that "will," in the language of modern metaphysics, does not mean only human willing, but that "will" and "willing" are the name of the Being of beings as a whole. Nietzsche's description of revenge as "the will's revulsion" brings revenge into relatedness with the Being of beings. That this is so becomes fully clear when we note what it is that the will's revulsion turns against. Revenge is—the will's revulsion against time and its "It was."

At first and second reading, and even still at a third reading, this definition of the essential nature of revenge will strike us as surprising, incomprehensible, and ultimately arbitrary. In fact, it must. It must do so as long as we overlook, first, the direction which the word "will" indicates here, and then, what the term "time" here means. But Nietzsche himself gives an answer to the question how he conceives time's essential nature. He says : Revenge is "the will's revulsion against time and its 'It was.' " We must think through this statement of Nietzsche with as much care as if we were dealing with one of Aristotle. And as concerns the definition of the essential nature of time, we are indeed faced with a statement of Aristotle. Of course, Nietzsche did not have Aristotle in mind when he wrote down his statement. Nor do we mean to suggest that Nietzsche is beholden to Aristotle. A thinker is not beholden to a thinker—rather, when he is thinking, he holds on to what is to be thought, to Being. Only insofar as he holds on to Being can he be open to the influx of the thoughts which thinkers before him have thought. This is why it remains the exclusive privilege of the greatest thinkers to let themselves be influenced. The small thinkers, by contrast, merely suffer from constipated originality, and hence close themselves off against any influx coming from afar. Nietzsche says : Revenge is "the will's revulsion against time . . . ."

He does not say: against something temporal; he does not say: against a specific characteristic of time; he says flatly: revulsion against time. Of course, the words "and its 'It was' " follow directly. That means, does it not: against the "it was" in time. We shall here be reminded that time includes not only the "it was," but also the "it will be" and the "it is now." Certainly. Time includes not only the past but also the future and the present. Nietzsche, then, by stressing the "it was," does intend time in a particular respect, and not "time" as such, in general. But what about "time"? After all it is not a bundle in which past, future, and present are wrapped up together. Time is not a cage in which the "no longer now," the "not yet now," and the "now" are cooped up together. How do matters stand with "time"? They stand thus: time goes. And it goes in that it passes away. The passing of time is, of course, a coming, but a coming which goes, in passing away. What comes in time never comes to stay, but to go. What comes in time always bears beforehand the mark of going past and passing away. This is why everything temporal is regarded simply as what is transitory. This is why the "It was" does not mention just one out of time's three sectors. Rather: the true endowment which time gives and leaves behind is what has passed away, the "It was." Time gives only what it has, and it has only what it is itself.

Therefore, when Nietzsche says that revenge is the will's revulsion against time and its "It was," he does not just single out some particular determinant of time, but he describes and defines time in respect of what distinguishes it in its total time character. And that is its passing away. The word "and" in Nietzsche's phrase "time and its 'It was' " is not just a conjunction to add some particular; this "and" here signifies as much as "and that means." Revenge is the will's revulsion against time, and that means, against the passing away and its past.

This characterization of time as a passing away, a flowing away in succession, the emergence and fading of every "now" that rolls past, out of the "not yet now" into the "no longer now"; the characterization, accordingly, of the temporal as the transitory—all this together is what marks the idea of "time" that is current throughout the metaphysics of the West.

Summary and Transition

"For that man be delivered from revenge: that is for me the bridge to the highest hope. . . ."

Whether this highest hope of which Nietzsche is thinking still leaves room for hope, or whether it does not on the contrary carry within itself the real devastation, is something we cannot make out as long as we fail to risk crossing over the bridge with Nietzsche. The crossing over the bridge, however, is not just one step in Nietzsche's thought among many others. This crossing of the bridge is the one real step, and here that means always the sole step, of the entire thinking in which Nietzsche's metaphysics is developed. The purpose of the present lecture is to help us join Nietzsche in this one step of his thought. The bridge is the deliverance from revenge. The bridge leads away from revenge. We ask: where? It leads where there is no more room for revenge. That cannot be just any place—nor is it. The passage across the bridge leads us to the peak of Nietzsche's metaphysics.

Deliverance from revenge remains from the outset partly determined by what revenge itself is. For Nietzsche, revenge is the fundamental characteristic of all thought so far. That is to say: revenge marks the manner in which man so far relates himself to what is. Nietzsche thinks of the nature of revenge in the light of this relation. Merely by relating himself to what is, man places and faces beings in their Being. Seen in the light of what is, the facing, the idea of beings always goes beyond beings. For instance, when we are facing the cathedral, we are faced not just with a church, a building, but with something that is present, in its presence. But the presence of what is present is not finally and *also* something we face, rather it comes before. Prior to all else it stands before us, only we do not see it because we stand within it. It is what really comes before us. The facing, the idea of what is, judged from what is, is always beyond what is—μετά. To have seen this μετά, that is, to have thought it, is the simple and thus inexhaustible meaning of all Greek thought. The idea of what is, is in itself metaphysical. When Nietzsche thinks of revenge as the fundamental characteristic of the way ideas have been formed so far, he thinks of revenge metaphysically—that is, not only psychologically, not only morally.

In modern metaphysics, the Being of beings appears as the will. "Willing is primal being," says Schelling. Among the long established predicates of primal being are "eternity and independence of time." Accordingly, only that will is primal being which as will is independent of time, and eternal. But that does not just mean the purely external indication that the will occurs constantly and independently of time. Eternal will does not mean only a will that lasts eternally: it says that will is primal being only when it is eternal as *will*. And it is that when, as will, it eternally wills the eternity of willing. The will that is eternal in this sense no longer follows and depends on the temporal in what it wills, or in its willing. It is independent of time. And so it can no longer be affronted by time.

Revenge, says Nietzsche, is the will's revulsion. What is refractory in revenge, what is revolting in it, is not, however, accomplished merely by a willing; rather, it is above all related to the will—in metaphysical terms, related to particular beings in their Being. That this is so becomes clear when we give thought to what it is *against* which the revulsion of revenge revolts. Nietzsche says: Revenge is the will's revulsion against time and its "It was." What does "time" mean here? Our closer reflection in the preceding lecture had this result: when Nietzsche, in his definition of the essential nature of revenge, mentions time, his idea of "time" is that by which the temporal is made the temporal. And what is temporal? We all know it without much cogitation. We are unmistakably reminded of what it is when we are told that someone's "time was up." The temporal is what must pass away. And time is the passing away of what must pass away. This passing away is conceived more precisely as the successive flowing away of the "now" out of the "not yet now" into the "no longer now." Time causes the passing away of what must pass away, and does so by passing away itself; yet it itself can pass away only if it persists throughout all the passing away. Time persists, consists in passing. It is, in that it constantly is not. This is the representational idea of time that characterizes the concept of "time" which is standard throughout the metaphysics of the West.

LECTURE
X

What is the origin of this long familiar idea of time as that which passes away, the temporal as what must pass away? Did this definition of time drop out of the sky, like an Absolute? Is it obvious merely because it has been current for so long? And how did this idea of time gain currency? How did it get into the current of Western thought?

It is time, it is high time finally to think through this nature of time, and its origin, so that we may reach the point where it becomes clear that all metaphysics leaves something essential unthought: its own ground and foundation. This is the ground on which we have to say that we are not yet truly thinking as long as we think only metaphysically. When metaphysics inquires into the nature of time, it will presumably, will necessarily have to, ask its questions in the way that is in keeping with its general manner of inquiry. Metaphysics asks: τί τὸ ὄν (Aristotle) : what is being? Starting from being, it asks for the Being of beings. What in beings is in being? In what does the Being of beings consist? With reference to time, this is to say: what of time is truly in being? In accordance with this manner of inquiry, time is conceived as something that in some way *is*, something that is in being, and so the question of its Being is raised. Aristotle, in his *Physics*, IV, 10–14,

100

has given a classic development of this manner of inquiry. And the answer Aristotle gave to the question of the essential nature of time still governs Nietzsche's idea of time. All subsequent conceptions of time have their roots in this basic, Aristotelian idea of time, which is implicit in Greek thought. That does not exclude, it includes the fact that individual thinkers such as Plotinus, Augustine, Leibniz, Kant, Hegel, and Schelling interpret the same situation in different directions. What is the situation in regard to time? What of time has being? As soon as metaphysical thought poses this question, it has already decided for itself what it understands by "in being," and in what sense it thinks the word "being." "In being" means: being present. Beings are more in being the more present they are. Beings come to be more present, the more abidingly they abide, the more lasting the abiding is. What in time is present, and therefore of the present? Only the "now" is of the present time at each given moment. The future *is* the "not yet now"; the past *is* the "no longer now." The future is what is still absent, the past what is already absent. In being, present in time at the given moment is only that narrow ridge of the momentary fugitive "now," rising out of the "not yet now" and falling away into the "no longer now." Today's reckoning in sports, for instance, with tenths of seconds, in modern physics even with millionths of seconds, does not mean that we have a keener grasp of time, and thus gain time; such reckoning is on the contrary the surest way to lose essential time, and so to "have" always less time. Thought out more precisely: the growing loss of time is not caused by such a time reckoning—rather, this time reckoning began at that moment when man suddenly became un-restful because he had no more time. That moment is the beginning of the modern age.

What in time is in being, present? The "now" of the given moment. But each "now" is in its present being by virtue of its passing. Future and past are *not* present, they are something of which we may never say simply that they are being present. According to Aristotle, therefore, the future and the past are a μὴ ὄν τι, and by no means an οὐκ ὄν, something that is entirely without being, they are something that lacks presence. Augustine says exactly the same thing, for example, in a commentary on the Thirty-Eighth Psalm: *Nihil de praeterito revocatur, quod futurum est, transiturum expectatur* (Nothing of what has passed will be called back, what is of the future is expected as something that will pass by). And later in the same passage, he almost follows Aristotle verbatim when he says: *et est et non est* (Migne, IV, 419a). The essential nature of time is here conceived in the light of Being and, let us note it well, of a totally specific interpretation of "Being"—Being as being present. This interpretation of Being has been current so long that we regard it as self-evident.

Since in all metaphysics from the beginning of Western thought, Being means being present, Being, if it is to be thought in the highest instance, must be thought as pure presence, that is, as the presence that persists, the abiding present, the steadily standing "now." Medieval thought speaks of *nunc stans*. But that is the interpretation of the nature of eternity.

Here let us recall for a moment the explanation Schelling adds to the statement "willing is primal being." He says that among the predicates of primal being there are "eternity, independence of time."

If all metaphysics thinks of Being as eternity and independence of time, it means precisely this: the idea of beings sees them as in their Being independent of time, the idea of time sees time in the sense of a passing away. What must pass away cannot be the ground of the eternal. To be properly beings in their Being means to be independent of time in the sense of a passing away. But what about that definition, here left unattended, of Being itself as being present, even as the enduring presence? What about Being as the being-present, in whose light time was conceived as a passing away, and even eternity as the present "now"? Is not this definition of Being ruled by the view of presence, the present—ruled, that is, by the view of time, and of a time of such a nature as we could never surmise, let alone think, with the help of the traditional time concept? What about Being and Time, then? Must not one as much as the other, Being as much as Time—must not both become questionable in their relatedness, first questionable and finally doubtful? And does not this show, then, that something was left unthought at the very core of the definition which is regarded as guiding all Western metaphysics—something essential in the essential nature of Being? The question "Being and Time" points to what is unthought in all metaphysics. Metaphysics consists of this unthought matter; what is unthought in metaphysics is therefore not a defect of metaphysics. Still less may we declare metaphysics to be false, or even reject it as a wrong turn, a mistake, on the grounds that it rests upon this unthought matter.

Revenge, for Nietzsche, is the will's revulsion against time. This now means: revenge is the will's revulsion against the passing away and what has passed away, against time and its "It was." The revulsion turns not against the mere passing, but against that passing away which allows what has passed to be only in the past, which lets it freeze in the finality of this *rigor mortis*. The revulsion of revenge is against that time which makes everything dissolve in the "It was," and thus makes passing pass away. The revulsion of revenge is not against the mere passing of time, but against the time that makes the passing pass away in the past, against the "It was." The revulsion of revenge remains chained to this "It was"; just as there lies concealed in all hatred the abysmal dependence upon that from which

hatred at bottom always desires to make itself independent
—but never can, and can all the less the more it hates.

What, then, is the deliverance from revenge, if revenge
chains man to the arrested past? Deliverance is the detach-
ment from what is revolting to the revulsion of revenge.
Deliverance from revenge is not liberation from all will.
For, since will is Being, deliverance as the annulment of
willing would lead to nothingness. Deliverance from revenge is the will's liberation from what is revolting to it, so
that the will can at last be will.

At what point is this "It was" removed which is always
revolting to the will? Not when there is no longer any passing away at all. For us men, time cannot be removed. But
what is revolting to the will fades away when the past does
not freeze in the mere "It was," to confront willing in fixed
rigidity. What is revolting vanishes when the passing is
not just a letting-pass in which the past sinks away into the
mere "It was." The will becomes free from what revolts it
when it becomes free as will, that is, free for the going in
the passing away—but the kind of going that does not get
away from the will, but comes back, bringing back what is
gone. The will becomes free from its revulsion against time,
against time's mere past, when it steadily wills the going
and coming, this going and coming back, of everything.
The will becomes free from what is revolting in the "It
was" when it wills the constant recurrence of every "It
was." The will is delivered from revulsion when it wills the
constant recurrence of the same. Then the will wills the
eternity of what is willed. The will wills its own eternity.
Will is primal being. The highest product of primal being
is eternity. The primal being of beings is the will, as the
eternally recurrent willing of the eternal recurrence of the
same. The eternal recurrence of the same is the supreme
triumph of the metaphysics of the will that eternally wills
its own willing. Deliverance from revenge is the transition,

from the will's revulsion against time and its "It was," to the will that eternally wills the recurrence of the same and in this willing wills itself as its own ground. Deliverance from revenge is the transition to the primal being of all beings.

At this point a remark must be inserted which, however, will have to remain just a remark. As the will of the eternal recurrence of the same, the will can will in reverse. For it will never encounter in that direction any fixed bygones that it could no longer will. The will of the eternal recurrence of the same frees willing of any possibility to encounter anything revolting. For the will of the eternal recurrence of the same wills the reverse from the start and entire—it wills return and recurrence. Christian dogma knows of another way in which the "It was" may be willed back—repentance. But repentance takes man where it is meant to take him, to the deliverance from the "It was," only if it maintains its essential relation to the forgiveness of sin, and thus is generally and from the outset referred to sin. Sin, however, is essentially different from moral failure. Sin exists only in the sphere of faith. Sin is the lack of faith, the revolt against God as the Redeemer. If repentance, joined to the forgiveness of sin and only that way, can will the return of the past, this will of repentance, seen in the terms of thinking, is always determined metaphysically, and is possible only that way—possible only by its relation to the eternal will of the redeeming God. If Nietzsche does not take the Christian road of repentance, it is because of his interpretation of Christianity and what it means to be a Christian. This interpretation in turn is based on his understanding of revenge and what it means for all representation. And Nietzsche's interpretation of revenge is based on the fact that he thinks of all things in their relatedness to Being as will.

Deliverance from revenge is the bridge crossed by him

who goes across. Where does he go, he who goes across? He goes where there is no more room for revenge as the revulsion against what merely passes away. He who goes across goes toward the will that wills the eternal recurrence of the same, toward the will which, being this will, is the primal being of all beings.

The superman surpasses man as he is by entering into the relatedness to Being—Being which, as the will of the eternal recurrence of the same, eternally wills itself and nothing else. The superman goes toward the eternal recurrence of the same, because that is where his essential nature is rooted. Nietzsche casts the superman's being in the figure of Zarathustra. Who is Zarathustra? He is the teacher of the eternal recurrence of the same. The metaphysics of the Being of beings, in the sense of the eternal recurrence of the same, is the ground and foundation of the book *Thus Spoke Zarathustra*. Even in the early drafts for Part IV and the conclusion of the work, dating from 1883, Nietzsche says it clearly (WW XII, 397, 399, 401) : "Zarathustra proclaims the doctrine of recurrence." "Zarathustra, *out of the superman's happiness, tells the secret* that everything recurs."

Zarathustra teaches the doctrine of the superman because he is the teacher of the eternal recurrence of the same. Zarathustra teaches both doctrines "at once" (XII, 401), because in their essence they belong together. Why do they belong together? Not because they are these particular doctrines, but because in both doctrines there is thought at the same time that which belongs together from the beginning and thus inevitably must be thought together—the Being of beings and its relatedness to the nature of man.

But this relatedness of Being to man's nature, as the relation of that nature to Being, has not yet been given thought in respect of its essential nature and origin. Hence we are still not able even to give to all this an adequate and fitting name. But because the relation between Being and human nature carries all things, in that it brings Being's appearance as well as man's essential nature to fruition, therefore the relation must find expression at the very beginning of Western metaphysics. The relation is mentioned in the principal statements made by Parmenides and Heraclitus. What they tell us does not just stand at the beginning, it is the beginning of Western thought itself—a beginning that we still conceive in an all too artless, all too uninitiated fashion, only as a part of history.

Both Nietzsche's doctrine of the eternal recurrence of the same, and his doctrine of the superman, must be traced back in thought to the relation between Being and human nature, so that we can give thought to both on their own doubt-provoking common grounds. Only then can we fully fathom what it means to say that Nietzsche's interpretation of the nature of revenge is metaphysical. The nature of revenge as will, and as revulsion against the passing away, is conceived in the light of will as primal being—the will which wills itself eternally as the eternal recurrence of the same. This is the thought which carries and determines the inner movement of the work *Thus Spoke Zarathustra*. The work moves in the style of a steadily increasing hesitation and *ritardando*. That style is not a literary device; it is nothing less than the thinker's relatedness to the Being of beings, which must find expression. Nietzsche had the thought of the eternal recurrence of the same even when he wrote his *Joyful Knowledge*, published in 1882. In the next-to-last section (341), "The Greatest Stress," the thought is expressed for the first time; the last section, *"Incipit tragoedia,"* already includes the beginning of the first part of *Thus Spoke Zarathustra* which was to appear the following year. Yet, in this book, that sustaining thought is not expressed until Part III—not that Nietzsche had not yet thought of it when he wrote Parts I and II. The thought of the eternal recurrence of the same is mentioned immediately at the beginning of Part III, in the second section which for good reasons is entitled "On the Vision and the Riddle." However, the preceding Part II had concluded with the section "The Stillest Hour," where it says: "Then it spoke to me again without voice: 'What do you matter, Zarathustra? Speak your word and break!' " The thought of the eternal recurrence of the same is Nietzsche's weightiest thought in a twofold sense; it is the most strenuous to think, and it has the greatest weight. It is the heaviest thought to bear. And while we must guard in every respect against taking this weightiest thought of Nietzsche too lightly, we still will ask: does the thought of the eternal recurrence of the same, does the recurrence itself bring with it deliverance from revenge?

There is a note which, to judge by the handwriting, dates from 1885 or at the latest 1886, with the (underscored) title "Recapitulation." It is a resume and gathering together of Nietzsche's metaphysics and is included in *The Will to Power* as #617. It says: "That *everything recurs* is the extremest *approximation of a world of Becoming to the world of Being:—the high point of meditation.*"

But that high point does not rise with clear, firm outlines into the brightness of translucent ether. The peak remains wrapped in thick clouds—not just for us, but for Nietzsche's own thinking. The reasons do not lie in any inability of Nietzsche, although his various attempts to demonstrate that the eternal recurrence of the same was the Being of all becoming led him curiously astray. It is the matter itself which is named by the term "the eternal recurrence of the same" that is wrapped in a darkness from which even Nietzsche had to shrink back in terror. In the earliest preliminary sketches for Part IV of *Thus Spoke Zarathustra* there is found a notation which truly contains the motto for the kind of writings that Nietzsche himself published after Zarathustra.

There it says: "We did create the heaviest thought—
now let us create the being to whom it will be light and
blissful! . . . To celebrate the future, not the past. To
write the mythos of the future! To live in hope! Blissful
moments! And then to draw the curtain shut again, and
turn *our thoughts* to firm and present purposes!" (XII,
400).

The thought of the eternal recurrence of the same remains veiled—and not just by a curtain. However, the
darkness of this last thought of Western metaphysics must
not mislead us, must not prompt us to avoid it by subterfuge. Fundamentally there are only two subterfuges.
Either we say that this Nietzschean thought of the eternal
recurrence of the same is a kind of mysticism and does not
belong in the court of thought. Or else we say: this thought
is already as old as the hills, and amounts to the cyclical
world view, which can be found in Heraclitus' fragments
and elsewhere. This second bit of information, like everything of its kind, says absolutely nothing. What good is it
supposed to do us to ascertain that some thought can
"already" be found in Leibniz, or even "already" in Plato
—if Leibniz' thought and Plato's thought are left in the
same darkness as this thought that is allegedly clarified by
such references!

But as concerns the first subterfuge, according to which
Nietzsche's thought of the eternal recurrence of the same
is a mystical fantasy: The coming age, in which the essence
of modern technology—the steadily rotating recurrence of
the same—will come to light, might have taught man that
a thinker's essential thoughts do not become in any way
less true simply because we fail to think them.

With his thought of the eternal recurrence of the same,
Nietzsche thinks what Schelling speaks of when he tells us
that all philosophy strives to find the highest expression for
primal being as the will. One thing remains, however, to
which every thinker must give thought. Nietzsche's at-

tempt to think the Being of beings makes it almost obtru-
sively clear to us moderns that all thinking, that is, relatedness to Being, is still difficult. Aristotle describes this
difficulty as follows (*Metaphysics*, Ch. 1, Bk. 2, 993b) :

"ὥσπερ γὰρ τὰ τῶν νυκτερίδων ὄμματα πρὸς τὸ
φέγγος ἔχει τὸ μεθ' ἡμέραν, οὕτω καὶ τῆς ἡμετέρας
ψυχῆς ὁ νοῦς πρὸς τὰ τῇ φύσει φανερώτατα πάντων."

"Just as it is with bats' eyes in respect of daylight, so it is
with our mental vision in respect of those things which are
by nature most apparent" (that is, the presence of all that
is present). The Being of beings is the most apparent; and
yet, we normally do not see it—and if we do, only with
difficulty.

PART

———◆———

TWO

LECTURE

I

———◆———

What is called thinking? The question sounds definite. It seems unequivocal. But even a slight reflection shows it to have more than one meaning. No sooner do we ask the question than we begin to vacillate. Indeed, the ambiguity of the question foils every attempt to push toward the answer without some further preparation.

We must, then, clarify the ambiguity. The ambiguousness of the question, "What is called thinking?", conceals several possible ways of dealing with it. Getting ahead of ourselves, we may stress *four* ways in which the question can be posed.

"What is called thinking?" says for one thing, and in the first place: what is it we call "thought" and "thinking," what do these words signify? What is it to which we give the name "thinking"?

"What is called thinking?" says also, in the second place: how does traditional doctrine conceive and define what we have named thinking? What is it that for two and a half thousand years has been regarded as the basic characteristic of thinking? Why does the traditional doctrine of thinking bear the curious title "logic"?

"What is called thinking?" says further, in the third place: what are the prerequisites we need so that we may be

113

able to think with essential rightness? What is called for on our part in order that we may each time achieve good thinking?

"What is called thinking?" says finally, in the fourth place: what is it that calls us, as it were, commands us to think? What is it that calls us into thinking?

These are four ways in which we can ask the question, and bring it closer to an answer by corresponding analyses. These four ways of asking the question are not just superficially strung together. They are all interrelated. What is disturbing about the question, therefore, lies less in the multiplicity of its possible meanings than in the single meaning toward which all four ways are pointing. We must consider whether only one of the four ways is the right one, while the others prove to be incidental and untenable; or whether all four of them are equally necessary because they are unified and of a piece. But how are they unified, and by what unity? Is oneness added to the multiplicity of the four ways as a fifth piece, like a roof to four walls? Or does one of the four ways of asking the question take precedence? Does this precedence establish a rank order within the group of questions? Does the rank order exhibit a structure by which the four ways are coordinated and yet subordinated to the one that is decisive?

The four ways we have mentioned, in which the question "What is called thinking?" may be asked, do not stand side by side, separate and unrelated. They belong together by virtue of a union that is enjoined by one of the four ways. However, we must go slow, one step at a time, if we are to become aware how this is so. We must therefore begin our attempt with a statement which will at first remain a mere assertion. It runs:

The meaning of the question which we noted in the fourth place tells us how the question would want to be asked first in the decisive way. "What is called thinking— what does call for thinking?" Properly understood, the question asks what it is that commands us to enter into thought, that calls on us to think. The turn of phrase, "What does call for thinking?," could of course intend no more than "what does the term 'thinking' signify to us?" But the question as it is really asked, "what does call for thinking on our part?," means something else. It means: what is it that directs us into thought, and gives us directions for thinking?

Accordingly, does the question ask what it is that gives us the impetus to think on each occasion and with regard to a particular matter? No. The directions that come from what directs us into thought are much more than merely the given impetus to do some thinking.

That which directs us to think, gives us directions in such a way that we first become capable of thinking, and thus *are* as thinkers, only by virtue of its directive. It is true, of course, that the question "What does call for thinking?," in the sense of "What calls on us to think?," is foreign to the common understanding. But we are all the less entitled simply to overlook the fact that the question "What is called thinking?" presents itself at first quite innocently. It sounds as if, and we unknowingly take it as if, the question merely asked for more precise information about what is supposedly meant when we speak of such a thing as thinking. Thinking here appears as a theme with which one might deal as with any other. Thus thinking becomes the object of an investigation. The investigation considers a process that occurs in man. Man takes a special part in the process, in that he performs the thinking. Yet this fact, that man is naturally the performer of thinking, need not further concern the investigation of thinking. The fact goes without saying. Being irrelevant, it may be left out of our reflection on thinking. Indeed, it must be left out. For the laws of thought are after all valid independently of the man who performs the individual acts of thinking.

But if the question "What does call for thinking?" is

asking what it is that first of all directs us to think, then we are asking for something that concerns ourselves because it calls upon us, upon our very being. It is we ourselves to whom the question "What is called thinking—what does call for thinking?" is addressed directly. We ourselves are in the text and texture of the question. The question "What calls on us to think?" has already drawn us into the substance of the inquiry. We ourselves are, in the strict sense of the word, put in question by the question. The question "What calls on us to think?" strikes us directly, like a lightning bolt. Asked in this way, the question "What does thinking call for?" does more than merely struggle with an object, in the manner of a scientific problem.

This other formulation of the question, which strikes us as strange, is open to the following immediate objection. The new meaning of the question "What does call for thinking?" has been obtained here by arbitrarily forcing on the question a signification totally different from the one that all the world would attach to it on hearing or reading it. This trick is easily exposed. It obviously relies on a mere play with words. And the victim of the play is the word which, as the verb of the question, sustains the sentence "What is called thinking?" We are playing with the verb "to call."

One might ask, for instance: "What do you call that village up there on the hill?" We want to know the name of the village. Or we may ask: "What shall we call the child?" That says: what name shall it bear? "What is called thinking?" means, then, what idea shall we form about the process to which has been given the name "thinking"? This is how we understand the question if we take it simply and naturally.

But if we are to hear the question in a sense which asks for what it is that directs us to think, we find ourselves suddenly compelled to accept the verb "to call" in a signification that is strange to us, or at least no longer familiar.

We are now supposed to use the word "to call" in a signification which one might paraphrase approximately with the verbs "invite, demand, instruct, direct." We call on someone who is in our way to give way, to make room. But the "call" does not necessarily imply demand, still less command; it rather implies an anticipatory reaching out for something that is reached by our call, through our calling.

In the widest sense, "to call" means to set in motion, to get something underway—which may be done in a gentle and therefore unobtrusive manner, and in fact is most readily done that way. In the older Greek version of the New Testament, Matthew 8:18, we find: "Ἰδὼν δὲ ὁ Ἰησοῦς ὄχλον περὶ αὐτὸν ἐκέλευσεν ἀπελθεῖν εἰς τὸ πέραν—Seeing a large crowd around him, he called to them to go to the other side." The Greek verb κελεύειν properly means to get something on the road, to get it underway. The Greek noun κέλευθος means way. And that the old word "to call" means not so much a command as a letting-reach, that therefore the "call" has an assonance of helpfulness and complaisance, is shown by the fact that the same word in Sanskrit still means something like "to invite."

The meaning of the word "call" which we have described is thus not altogether unfamiliar to us. It still is unaccustomed as we encounter it in the question "What is called thinking—what does call for it?" When we hear that question, the meaning of "call" in the sense of "instruct, demand, allow to reach, get on the way, convey, provide with a way" does not immediately occur to us. We are not so much at home with these meanings of the word that we hear them at first, let alone first of all. We do not have the habit, or only just barely, of using the word "call" in this sense. And so it remains unfamiliar to us. Instead, we follow the habitual signification of the verb "to call," and mostly stay within it, not giving it much thought. "To call" just simply means to give this or that name. In that signification, the word is current among us. And why do we prefer the customary meaning, even unknowingly? Presumably because the unaccustomed and apparently uncustomary signification of the word "to call" is its proper one: the one that is innate to the word, and thus remains the only one—for from its native realm stem all the other.

"To call," in short, means "to command," provided we hear this word, too, in its native, telling sense. For "to command" basically means, not to give commands and orders, but to commend, entrust, give into safe-keeping, keep safely. To call means: to call into arrival and presence; to address commendingly.

Accordingly, when we hear our question "What is called thinking?" in the sense that it asks, What is it that appeals to us to think?, we then are asking: What is it that enjoins our nature to think, and thus lets our nature reach thought, arrive in thinking, there to keep it safe?

When we ask in this way we do, of course, use the word "to call" in a rather unfamiliar signification. But it is unhabitual not because our spoken speech has never yet been at home in it, but rather because *we* are no longer at home with this telling word, because we no longer really live in it.

We turn back to the originally habitual significance of the word "to call," and ask: "What is it that calls on us to think?"

Is this return a whim, or playing games? Neither one nor the other. If we may talk here of playing games at all, it is not we who play with words, but the nature of language plays with us, not only in this case, not only now, but long since and always. For language plays with our speech—it likes to let our speech drift away into the more obvious meanings of words. It is as though man had to make an effort to live properly with language. It is as though such a dwelling were especially prone to succumb to the danger of commonness.

The place of language properly inhabited, and of its habitual words, is usurped by common terms. The common speech becomes the current speech. We meet it on all sides, and since it is common to all, we now accept it as the only standard. Anything that departs from this commonness, in order to inhabit the formerly habitual proper speech of language, is at once considered a violation of the standard. It is branded as a frivolous whim. All this is in fact quite in order, as soon as we regard the common as the only legitimate standard, and become generally incapable of fathoming the commonness of the common. This floundering in a commonness which we have placed under the protection of so-called natural common sense, is not accidental, nor are we free to deprecate it. This floundering in commonness is part of the high and dangerous game and gamble in which, by the nature of language, we are the stakes.

Is it playing with words when we attempt to give heed to this game of language and to hear what language really says when it speaks? If we succeed in hearing that, then it may happen—provided we proceed carefully—that we get more truly to the matter that is expressed in any telling and asking.

We give heed to the real signification of the word "to call," and accordingly ask our question, "What does thinking call for?" in this way: what is it that directs us into thinking, that calls on us to think? But after all, the word "to call" means also, and commonly, to give a name to something. The current meaning of the word cannot simply be pushed aside in favor of the rare one, even though the rare signification may still be the real one. That would be an open violation of language. Besides, the presently more

current signification of the word "call" is not totally uncon-
nected and unrelated to the real one. On the contrary, the
presently customary signification is rooted in the other,
original, decisive one. For, what is it that the word "to
name" tells us?

When we name a thing, we furnish it with a name. But
what about this furnishing? After all, the name is not just
draped over the thing. On the other hand, no one will deny
that the name is coordinated with the thing as an object. If
we conceive the situation in this way, we turn the name,
too, into an object. We see the relation between name and
thing as the coordination of two objects. The coordination
in turn is by way of an object, which we can see and conceive and deal with and describe according to its various
possibilities. The relation between what is named and its
name can always be conceived as a coordination. The only
question is whether this correctly conceived coordination
will ever allow us, will allow us at all, to give heed to what
constitutes the peculiar property of the name.

To name something—that is to call it by name. More
fundamentally, to name is to call and clothe something
with a word. What is so called, is then at the call of the
word. What is called appears as what is present, and in its
presence it is brought into the keeping, it is commanded,
called into the calling word. So called by name, called into
a presence, it in turn calls. It is named, has the name. By
naming, we call on what is present to arrive. Arrive where?
That remains to be thought about. In any case, all naming
and all being named is the familiar "to call" only because
naming itself consists by nature in the real calling, in the
call to come, in a commending and a command.

What is called thinking? At the outset we mentioned
four ways to ask the question. We said that the way listed
in the fourth place is the first, first in the sense of being

highest in rank since it sets the standard. When we understand the question, "What is called thinking?," in the sense that it is a question about what calls upon us to think, we then have understood the word "to call" in its proper significance. That is to say also: we now ask the question as it properly wants to be asked. Presumably we shall now almost automatically get to the three remaining ways to ask the question. It will therefore be advisable to explicate the real question a little more clearly. It runs: "What is it that calls on us to think?" What makes a call upon us that we should think and, by thinking, be who we are?

That which calls us to think in this way presumably can do so only insofar as the calling itself, on its own, needs thought. What calls us to think, and thus commands, that is, brings our essential nature into the keeping of thought, needs thinking because what calls us wants itself to be thought about according to its nature. What calls on us to think, demands for itself that it be tended, cared for, husbanded in its own essential nature, by thought. What calls on us to think, gives us food for thought.

What gives us food for thought we call thought-provoking. But what is thought-provoking not just occasionally, and not just in some given limited respect, but rather gives food for thought inherently and hence from the start and always—is that which is thought-provoking *per se*. This is what we call most thought-provoking. And what it gives us to think about, the gift it gives to us, is nothing less than itself—itself which calls on us to enter thought.

The question "What is called thinking?" asks for what wants to be thought about in the pre-eminent sense: it does not just give us something to think about, nor only itself, but it first gives thought and thinking to us, it entrusts thought to us as our essential destiny, and thus first joins and appropriates us to thought.

Summary and Transition

The question "What is called thinking?" can be asked in four ways. It asks:

1. What is designated by the word "thinking?"

2. What does the prevailing theory of thought, namely logic, understand by thinking?

3. What are the prerequisites we need to perform thinking rightly?

4. What is it that commands us to think?

We assert: the fourth question must be asked first. Once the nature of thinking is in question, the fourth is the decisive question. But this is not to say that the first three questions stand apart, outside the fourth. Rather, they point to the fourth. The first three questions subordinate themselves to the fourth which itself determines the structure within which the four ways of asking belong together.

We might say also: the fourth question, What is it that calls on to think?, develops and explicates itself in such a way that it calls forth the other three. But how the four questions belong together within the decisive fourth question, that is something we cannot find out by ingenuity. It must reveal itself to us. And it will do so only if we let ourselves become involved in the questioning of the question. To do that, we must strike out on a way. The way seems to be implicit in the fact that the fourth question is the decisive one. And the way must set out from this question, since the other three, too, come down to it. Still, it is not at all certain whether we are asking the fourth question in the right way if we begin our questioning with it.

The thing that is in substance and by nature first, need not stand at the beginning—in fact, perhaps it cannot. The first and the beginning are not identical. We must therefore first explore the four ways in which the question may be asked. The fourth way will probably prove to be decisive; yet another way remains unavoidable, which we must first find and travel to get to the fourth, decisive one. This situation alone tells us that the for us decisive way of asking our question, "What is called thinking?," is still remote and seems almost strange to us. It becomes necessary, then, first to acquaint ourselves explicitly with the ambiguity of the question, not only to give attention to that ambiguity as such, but also in order that we may not take it too lightly, as a mere matter of linguistic expression.

The ambiguity of the question "What is called thinking?" lies in the ambiguity of the questioning verb "to call."

The frequent idiom "what we call" signifies: what we have just said is meant in substance in this or that way, is to be understood this way or that. Instead of "what we call," we also use the idiom "that is to say."

On a day of changeable weather, someone might leave a mountain lodge, alone, to climb a peak. He soon loses his way in the fog that has suddenly descended. He has no notion of what we call mountaineering. He does not know any of the things it calls for, all the things that must be taken into account and mastered.

A voice calls to us to have hope. It beckons us to hope, invites us, commends us, directs us to hope.

This town is called Freiburg. It is so named because that is what it has been called. This means: the town has been called to assume this name. Henceforth it is at the call of this name to which it has been commended. To call is not originally to name, but the other way around: naming is a kind of calling, in the original sense of demanding and commending. It is not that the call has its being in the name; rather every name is a kind of call. Every call implies an approach, and thus, of course, the possibility of giving a name. We might call a guest welcome. This does not mean that we attach to him the name "Welcome," but that we call him to come in and complete his arrival as a welcome friend. In that way, the welcome-call of the invitation to come in is nonetheless also an act of naming, a calling which makes the newcomer what we call a guest whom we are glad to see.

But calling is something else than merely making a sound. Something else, again essentially different from mere sound and noise, is the cry. The cry need not be a call, but may be: the cry of distress. In reality, the calling stems from the place to which the call goes out. The calling is informed by an original outreach toward. . . . This alone is why the call can make a demand. The mere cry dies away and collapses. It can offer no lasting abode to either pain or joy. The call, by contrast, is a reaching, even if it is neither heard nor answered. Calling offers an abode. Sound and cry and call must be clearly distinguished.

The call is the directive which, in calling to and calling upon, in reaching out and inviting, directs us toward an action or non-action, or toward something even more essential. In every calling, a call has already gathered. The calling is not a call that has gone by, but one that has gone out and as such is still calling and inviting; it calls even if it makes no sound.

As soon as we understand the word "to call" in its original root significance, we hear the question "What is called thinking?" in a different way. We then hear the question: "What is That which calls on us to think, in the sense that it originally directs us to thinking and thereby entrusts to us our own essential nature as such—which is insofar as it thinks?"

What is it that calls on us to think? As we develop the question, it asks: where does the calling come from that calls on us to think? In what does this calling consist? How can it make its claim on us? How does the calling reach us?

How does it reach down into our very nature, in order to demand from us that our nature be a thinking nature? What is our nature? Can we know it at all? If there can be no knowledge here, then in what way is our nature revealed to us? Perhaps in just this way, and only in this way, that we are called upon to think?

"What is it that calls on us to think?" We find that we ourselves are put in question, this question, as soon as we truly ask it, not just rattle it off.

But from what other source could the calling into thought come than from something that in itself needs thought, because the source of the calling wants to be thought about by its very nature, and not just now and then? That which calls on us to think and appeals to us to think, claims thought for itself and as its own, because in and by itself it gives food for thought—not just occasionally but now and always.

What so gives food for thought is what we call most thought-provoking. Nor does it give only what always remains to be thought about; it gives food for thought in the much wider-reaching and decisive sense that it first entrusts thought and thinking to us as what determines our nature.

LECTURE

II

———————

What is most thought-provoking gives food for thought in the original sense that it gives us over, delivers us to thought. This gift, which gives to us what is most thought-provoking, is the true endowment that keeps itself concealed in our essential nature.

When we ask, then, "What is it that calls on us to think?," we are looking both to what it is that gives to us the gift of this endowment, and to ourselves, whose nature lies in being gifted with this endowment. We *are capable* of thinking only insofar as we *are* endowed with what is most thought-provoking, gifted with what ever and always wants to be thought about.

Whether we are in any given case capable of thinking, that is, whether we accomplish it in the fitting manner, depends on whether we are inclined to think, whether, that is, we will let ourselves become involved with the nature of thinking. It could be that we incline too slightly and too rarely to let ourselves become so involved. And that is so not because we are all too indolent, or occupied with other matters and disinclined to think, but because the involvement with thought is in itself a rare thing, reserved for few people.

What we have said must for the moment be sufficient explanation of the fourth way in which we ask the question "What is called thinking?" in the decisive way. However, our explanation has itself constantly been talking about thinking. We already have, then, an understanding of the words "thought" and "thinking" in their broad outlines, even if it be only the vague meaning that by thinking we understand something that is done by an act of the human spirit. We speak of acts of will, but also of acts of thought.

Precisely when we ask, "What is it that calls on us to think?," we reflect not only on the source of the calling, but with equal resolution on *what* it calls on us to do—we reflect on thinking. Thus, when we are called upon, we are not only commanded and called upon to do something, but that something itself is named in the call. In the wording of the question, the word "think" is not just a sound. All of us have already had some ideas about the word "think," however vague. True, all of us should be greatly embarrassed if we had to say, straight out and unequivocally, what it is that the verb "to think" designates. But, luckily, we do not have to say, we only are supposed to let ourselves become *involved* in the question. And if we do, we are already asking: what is it to which the word "thinking" gives a name? Having started with the decisive fourth question, we find ourselves involved in the first question as well.

What is it to which the word "thinking" gives a name? We hear the words "think," "thought," "thinking." As the saying goes, we attach a meaning to them. What comes to our minds here is at first fleeting and blurred. Most of the time, we can leave it at that. It satisfies the demands of common speech in usual communication. Such communication does not want to lose time tarrying over the sense of individual words. Instead, words are constantly thrown around on the cheap, and in the process are worn out. There is a curious advantage in that. With a worn-out language everybody can talk about everything.

But what if we ask specifically what it is to which the

word, here the word "thinking," gives a name? Then we attend to the word as word. This is what happened earlier with the word "to call." We are here venturing into the gambling game of language, where our nature is at stake. Nor can we avoid that venture, once we have become aware that—and in what way—thought and poesy, each in its own unmistakable fashion, *are* the essential telling.

According to the common view, both thought and poesy use language merely as their medium and a means of expression, just as sculpture, painting, and music operate and express themselves in the medium of stone and wood and color and tone. But presumably stone and wood and color and tone, too, exhibit a different nature in art, once we get over seeing art aesthetically, that is, from the point of view of expression and impression—the work as expression, and the impression as experience.

Language is neither merely the field of expression, nor merely the means of expression, nor merely the two jointly. Thought and poesy never just use language to express themselves with its help; rather, thought and poesy are in themselves the originary, the essential, and therefore also the final speech that language speaks through the mouth of man.

To speak language is totally different from employing language. Common speech merely employs language. This relation to language is just what constitutes its commonness. But because thought and, in a different way poesy, do not employ terms but speak words, therefore we are compelled, as soon as we set out upon a way of thought, to give specific attention to what the word says.

At first, words may easily appear to be terms. Terms, in their turn, first appear spoken when they are given voice. Again, this is at first a sound. It is perceived by the senses. What is perceived by the senses is considered as immediately given. The word's signification attaches to its sound.

That constituent of the word—signification—cannot be perceived by the senses. What is non-sensual in the terms is their sense, their signification. Accordingly, we speak of sense-giving acts that furnish the word-sound with a sense. Terms thus become either full of sense, or more meaningful. The terms are like buckets or kegs out of which we can scoop sense.

Our scientifically organized dictionaries list these vessels of sense in alphabetical order, each entered and described according to its two constituents, sound-structure and sense-content. When we are specially concerned with what the word tells us, we stay with our dictionaries. This is how things look at first. Indeed, this "at first" does on the whole and from the start determine the idea we have of the usual ways of being concerned with the word. On the strength of this idea, we then judge the procedure of any thinking that is concerned with the word. We judge the procedure now favorably, now unfavorably, but always with reservations. Whatever our judgments may turn out to be, they are all baseless as long as it is not clear by what they are supported. For they are in fact supported by that "at first" which looks on terms as terms, not just at first but always, which looks on them, that is, as kegs and buckets. What about this much-invoked "at first"?

What we encounter at first is never what is near, but always only what is common. It possesses the unearthly power to break us of the habit of abiding in what is essential, often so definitively that we never come to abide anywhere.

When we hear directly what is spoken directly, we do not at first hear the words as terms, still less the terms as mere sound. In order to hear the pure resonance of a mere sound, we must first remove ourselves from the sphere where speech meets with understanding or lack of understanding. We must disregard all that, abstract from it, if we are to extract, subtract only the sound and resonance from what is spoken, if our ears are to catch this abstraction by itself, purely acoustically. Sound, which in the conceptual field of this supposed "at first" is regarded as immediately given, is an abstract construct that is at no time perceived alone, by itself, nor ever at first, when we hear something spoken.

The supposedly purely sensual aspect of the word-sound, conceived as mere resonance, is an abstraction. The mere vibration is always picked out only by an intermediate step —by that almost unnatural disregard. Even when we hear speech in a language totally unknown to us, we never hear mere sounds as a noise present only to our senses—we hear unintelligible words. But between the unintelligible word, and the mere sound grasped in acoustic abstraction, lies an abyss of difference in essence.

Nor are mere terms given at first when we hear speech. As hearers, we abide in the sphere of what is spoken, where the voice of what is said rings without sound. From this sphere, whose essential nature we have barely caught sight of, much less thought about, the words disclose themselves which speak in what is spoken, and which simply do not stand out individually.

Words are not terms, and thus are not like buckets and kegs from which we scoop a content that is there. Words are wellsprings that are found and dug up in the telling, wellsprings that must be found and dug up again and again, that easily cave in, but that at times also well up when least expected. If we do not go to the spring again and again, the buckets and kegs stay empty, or their content stays stale.

To pay heed to what the words say is different in essence from what it first seems to be, a mere preoccupation with terms. Besides, to pay heed to what the words say is particularly difficult for us moderns, because we find it hard to detach ourselves from the "at first" of what is common; and if we succeed for once, we relapse all too easily.

And so, even this excursus on word and terms will hardly prevent our taking the question, "What is called thinking?" meaning "What is it that the word 'thinking' calls by name?," at first in a superficial sense. The attempt to give heed to what the verb "think" tells us, will strike us as an empty, pointless dissection of terms picked at random, whose significance is tied to no tangible subject matter. There are reasons why this stubborn appearance will not fade, reasons to which we must give attention because they are deeply rooted and affect every explication and discussion of language.

If we ask what the word "thinking" designates, we obviously must go back into the history of the word "thinking." In order to reach the realm of speech from which the words "thought" and "thinking" speak, we must become involved with the history of language. That history has been made accessible by the scientific study of languages.

But attention to what words tell us is supposedly the decisive step and directive on that way of thinking which is known by the name philosophy. And can philosophy be based on the explication of terms, that is, on historical insights? That would seem even less possible than the attempt to prove the proposition "$2 \times 2 = 4$" by an opinion poll which ascertains that, as far as can be observed, men do indeed always assert that two times two equals four.

Philosophy cannot be based on history—neither on the science of history nor on any other science. For every science rests on presuppositions which can never be established scientifically, though they can be demonstrated philosophically. All sciences are grounded in philosophy, but not *vice versa*.

According to this reflection, philosophy is prevented from securing an alleged foundation for itself by way of an explanation of the meaning of words. Such explanations rely upon the history of language. They proceed historically. Knowledge of history, like all knowledge of matters of fact, is only conditionally certain, not unconditionally. All such knowledge has this limitation, that its statements are valid only so long as no new facts become known which compel the retraction of earlier statements. But philosophy is that supra-historical knowledge which, ever since Descartes, claims unconditional certainty for its tenets.

This reflection, often advanced and seemingly convincing, confounds various trains of thought and their various levels. This lecture course need not untangle the confusion, since along its own way it makes clear, though only indirectly, the relation between philosophy and the sciences.

Summary and Transition

It takes us a while to accept the multiplicity of meanings of the question "What is called thinking?" The question is fourfold. But it stems from a oneness, a simplicity. Accordingly, it does not break up into a chance multiplicity. Simplicity introduces measure and structure, and also initial power and endurance, into the four modes in which the question may be asked. The decisive mode is the fourth: what is it that calls on us to think? The calling makes us think what is most thought-provoking. The call endows us with thinking as the dowry of our nature. Through the call, then, man is in a way already informed of what the word "thinking" means. As soon as we ask the question, "What of that call which calls on us to think?," we find ourselves directed toward the question, "What does the verb 'to think' tell us?" We can no longer use the word at random, in some signification picked out of the air, around which we then build up a concept upon which to construct a theory of thinking. If we did, everything would be abandoned to caprice. The call to think determines what the word "to think" calls for. Yet the call which commends our nature to thought, is not a constraining force. The call sets our nature free, so decisively that only the calling which calls on us to think establishes the free scope of freedom in which free human nature may abide. The originary nature of freedom keeps itself concealed in the calling by which it is given to mortal man to think what is most thought-provoking. Freedom, therefore, is never something merely human, nor merely divine; still less is freedom the mere reflection of their belonging together.

As soon as the call calls on us to think, it has placed at our call what it calls for—thinking. What is called for now has a name, is called thus and so. What is that name which names what is called for? Surely the word "thinking."

However, this word "thinking," as it is sounded in speech, obviously belongs to one particular language. Thinking, however, is a matter common to all mankind. Now it is impossible to glean the nature of thinking from the mere signification of one solitary word in one particular language, and then to offer the result as binding. Surely not. The only thing we can glean that way is that something remains doubtful here. However: the same doubt affects the common, human, logical thinking—provided that henceforth we make up our minds no longer to ignore the fact that logic, all that belongs to *logos*, is also only a single word in the singular and particular language of the Greeks—and not just in its sound structure.

What does this word "thinking" say? Let us give close attention to what the words "thinking," "thought" have to tell. With these words something has entered language— not just of late, but long ago. But though it entered language, it did not get through. It has gone back into the unspoken, so that we cannot reach it without some further effort. In any event, if we are to give due attention to what has entered language with the words "thought" and "thinking," we must go back into the history of language. One of the ways that lead there is written history. By now it is a science, in our case the science of philology.

However, attention to what the words tell is here supposed to be a way for us to enter into thought. "Science does not think," we said in an earlier lecture. Science does not think in the sense in which thinkers think. Still, it does not at all follow that thinking need pay no attention to the sciences. The statement "science does not think" is not a license under which thinking is free to set itself up out of the blue, so to speak, simply by thinking something up.

Yet we have placed thinking close to poesy, and at a distance from science. Closeness, however, is something essentially different from the vacuous leveling of differences. The essential closeness of poesy and thinking is so far from excluding their difference that, on the contrary, it establishes that difference in an abysmal manner. This is something we moderns have trouble understanding.

For us, poesy has long since been a part of literature, and thinking likewise. We find it fitting that poesy and its history are dealt with in literary history. It would be foolish to find fault with this situation, which has reasons of long standing, or even to attempt changing it over night. And yet—Homer, Sappho, Pindar, Sophocles, are they literature? No! But that is the way they appear to us, and the only way, even when we are engaged in demonstrating by means of literary history that these works of poetry really are not literature.

Literature is what has been literally written down, and copied, with the intent that it be available to a reading public. In that way, literature becomes the object of widely diverging interests, which in turn are once more stimulated by means of literature—through literary criticism and promotion. Now and then, an individual may find his way out of the literature industry, and find his way reflectively and even edifyingly to a poetic work; but that is not enough to secure for poesy the freedom of its natural habitat. Besides, poesy must first itself determine and reach that habitat.

The poesy of the Occident and European literature are two radically different essential forces in our history. Our ideas of the nature and significance of literature are probably still totally inadequate.

However, through literature, and in literature as their medium, poesy and thought and science are assimilated to one another. If thinking is set over against science, it looks by scientific standards as if it were miscarried poesy. If, on the other hand, thinking knowingly avoids the vicinity of poesy, it readily appears as the super-science that would be more scientific than all the sciences put together.

But precisely because thinking does not make poetry, but is a primal telling and speaking of language, it must stay close to poesy. And since science does not think, thinking must in its present situation give to the sciences that searching attention which they are incapable of giving to themselves.

In saying this, we have mentioned only the lesser relatedness of thought to the sciences. The essential relatedness is determined rather by a basic trait of the modern era of which the literature we have referred to also forms a part. It might be briefly described as follows: that which is, appears today predominantly in *that* object-materiality which is established and maintained in power by the scientific objectification of all fields and areas. This materiality does not stem from a separate and peculiar power-bid on the part of the sciences, but from a fact in the nature of things that we moderns still do not want to see. Three propositions will serve to indicate it.

1. Modern science is grounded in the nature of technology.
2. The nature of technology is itself nothing technological.
3. The nature of technology is not a merely human fabrication which, given an appropriate moral con-

stitution, could be subdued by superior human wisdom and judgment.

We do not notice the scientific-literary objectification of that which is, simply because we are immersed in it. For that same reason, the relation of thinking to poesy and to science remains today utterly confused and in essence concealed, particularly since thinking itself is least familiar with the origin of its own essential nature. It would thus be possible to regard the question "What is called thinking?" merely as a well-chosen subject for the educational purposes of a lecture course. However, the question "What is called thinking?" is—if it is at all permissible to put this into words—a world-historical question. Usually, the name "world history" signifies the same thing as universal history. But in our usage, the word "world history" means the *fatum* that there *is* world, and that man *is* as its inhabitant. The world-historical question, "What is it that calls on us to think?" asks: That which really is—in what way does it come to touch the man of our era?

Our explication of the question has unexpectedly driven us to consider the relation of thinking to science. We are prompted by an obvious scruple, which can be briefly explained as follows. The question "What is called thinking?" unexpectedly assumes for us the mode we listed in the first place, which asks: what is it to which we give the name "thinking"? As we pursue it, we give attention to what the word says. This leads us to the history of the signification of terms. The history of language, however, is accessible only by historical investigation. And historical and philosophical knowledge, by an ancient doctrine, are radically different from each other.

Our concern with what words tell us, meanwhile, would secure solid grounds for the ways of thought. But can thinking, the philosophical, supra-historical knowledge of eternal truths, ever be grounded on historical findings?

This objection, which threatens our entire enterprise even in its first steps—how will we get it out of the way? We do not want at all to get this scruple out of the way. Let us, meanwhile, permit it to stand on the way on which it comes to meet us. For it could be that this way is no longer a way. Anyway, it might be considered advisable not to instigate a long-winded discussion of the relation between philosophy and science, until we have gone through at least a few steps of the question "What is called thinking?" And yet that question may even be such that it will never allow us to go through, but instead requires that we settle down and live within it.

LECTURE
III

———◆———

While trying to attend to what words can tell us, we let the relation to philology remain an open question. The findings of philology may in any case give us a clue on occasion. But this does not mean that the findings of philology, taken in themselves as the judgments of a science, must constitute the foundations on which we proceed. Whatever philology has to say must first be given to it historically; it must have reached philology by pre-scientific ways leading up to the history of language. Not until a history is already given, and only then, can the data of that history become the subject matter of written history, and even then the data always remain by their nature what they are. Here is where we take our clues.

In order to perceive a clue, we must first be listening ahead into the sphere from which the clue comes. To receive a clue is difficult, and rare—rarer the more we know, and more difficult the more we merely want to know. But clues also have forerunners, to whose directives we respond sooner and more easily, because we ourselves can help prepare them part of the way.

What is it that is named with the words "think," "thinking," "thought"? Toward what sphere of the spoken word do they direct us? A thought—where is it, where does it go? Thought is in need of memory, the gathering of thought.

The Old English *thencan*, to think, and *thancian*, to thank, are closely related; the Old English noun for thought is *thanc* or *thonc*—a thought, a grateful thought, and the expression of such a thought; today it survives in the plural *thanks*. The "thanc," that which is thought, the thought, implies the thanks. But perhaps these assonances between thought and thanks are superficial and contrived. In any case, they still do not show what is designated by the word "thinking."

Is thinking a giving of thanks? What do thanks mean here? Or do thanks consist in thinking? What does thinking mean here? Is memory no more than a container for the thoughts of thinking, or does thinking itself reside in memory? In asking these questions, we are moving in the area of those spoken words that speak to us from the verb "think." But let us leave open all the relationships between those words—"thinking," "thought," "thanks" and "memory"—and address our question now to the history of words. It gives us a direction, though the written account of that history is still incomplete, and presumably will always remain so.

We take the clue that in the speaking of those words the decisively and originally telling word is the "thanc." But this word does not mean the current meaning still left over in our present usage of the word "thought." A thought usually means an idea, a view or opinion, a notion. The root or originary word says: the gathered, all-gathering thinking that recalls. Thinking, in the sense of that telling root word "thanc," is almost closer to the origins than that thinking of the heart which Pascal, centuries later and even then in conscious opposition to mathematical thinking, attempted to retrieve.

Compared with the root *thanc*, thought in the sense of logical-rational representations turns out to be a reduction and an impoverishment of the word that beggar the imagination. Academic philosophy has done its share to stunt the

word—from which we may gather that conceptual definitions of terms, while necessary for technical and scientific
purposes, are by themselves unfit to assure, much less advance, the soundness of language, as they are generally
assumed to do.

But the word "*the thanc*" does not mean only what we
call a man's disposition or heart, and whose essential nature
we can hardly fathom. Both memory and thanks move and
have their being in the *thanc*. "Memory" initially did not
at all mean the power to recall. The word designates the
whole disposition in the sense of a steadfast intimate concentration upon the things that essentially speak to us in
every thoughtful meditation. Originally, "memory" means
as much as devotion: a constant concentrated abiding with
something—not just with something that has passed, but
in the same way with what is present and with what may
come. What is past, present, and to come appears in the
oneness of its own *present* being.

Inasmuch as memory—the concentration of our disposition, devotion—does not let go of that on which it con-
centrates, memory is imbued not just with the quality of
essential recall, but equally with the quality of an unrelin-
quishing and unrelenting retention. Out of the memory,
and within the memory, the soul then pours forth its wealth
of images—of visions envisioning the soul itself. Only now,
within the widely and deeply conceived nature of the
memory, the contrast emerges between oblivion and retention, what the Romans call *memoria tenere*. Retention by
memoria refers as much to what is past as to what is present
and to come. Retention is mostly occupied with what is past,
because the past has got away and in a way no longer
affords a lasting hold. Therefore, the meaning of retention
is subsequently limited to what is past, what memory draws
up, recovers again and again. But since this limited reference originally *does not* constitute the sole nature of memory, the need to give a name to the specific retention and

recovery of what is past gives rise to the coinage: re-calling memory—remembrance.

The originary word "thanc" is imbued with the original nature of memory: the gathering of the constant intention of everything that the heart holds in present being. Intention here is understood in this sense: the inclination with which the inmost meditation of the heart turns toward all that is in being—the inclination that is not within its own control and therefore also need not necessarily be first enacted as such.

The "thanc," being the memory so understood, is by the same token also what the word "thanks" designates. In giving thanks, the heart gives thought to what it has and what it is. The heart, thus giving thought and thus being memory, gives itself in thought to that to which it is held. It thinks of itself as beholden, not in the sense of mere submission, but beholden because its devotion is held in listening. Original thanking is the thanks owed for being. That thanks alone gives rise to thinking of the kind we know as retribution and reward in the good and bad sense. But thanking enacted by itself, as payment and repayment, remains too easily bogged down in the sphere of mere conventional recompense, even mere business.

Our attempt to indicate what the words "thinking," "thought," and "memory" say might serve to point at least vaguely toward the realm of speech from whose unspoken sphere those words initially speak. Those words bring to light situations whose essential unity of nature our eyes can not yet pierce. One thing remains obscure above all else. We can reduce it to the following question:

Does the characterization of *thanc*, memory, and thanks —not merely according to the words, but in substance— stem from thinking, or does thinking on the contrary receive its essential nature from the originary *thanc* as memory and thanking?

It may be that the question is posed altogether inadequately, so that nothing essential can be reached by way of it. Only this much is clear: what the words *thanc*, thought, memory, thanks designate is incomparably richer in essential content than the current signification that the words still have for us in common usage. We could rest satisfied with that observation. But not only do we now go beyond it; the attention we have given to what those words tell us has in advance prepared us to receive from their speaking a directive which carries us closer to the substance expressed in those words.

We shall accept the directive from the words "thinking," "*thanc*," "memory," and "thanks," taken in their originary sense, and shall try to discuss freely what the word "thinking" tells us in its richer language. Our discussion will be freer, not by being more unbounded, but because our vision achieves an open vista into the essential situations we have mentioned, and gains from them the possibility of an appropriate bond. Our more careful attention to what is named in the word "thinking" brings us directly from the first question to the decisive fourth.

The "*thanc*," as the original memory, is already pervaded by that thinking back which devotes what it thinks to that which is to be thought—it is pervaded by thanks. When we give thanks, we give it for something. We give thanks for something by giving thanks to him whom we have to thank for it. The things for which we owe thanks are not things we have from ourselves. They are given to us. We receive many gifts, of many kinds. But the highest and really most lasting gift given to us is always our essential nature, with which we are gifted in such a way that we are what we are only through it. That is why we owe thanks for this endowment, first and unceasingly.

But the thing given to us, in the sense of this dowry, is thinking. As thinking, it is pledged to what is there to be

thought. And the thing that of itself ever and anon gives
food for thought is what is the most thought-provoking. In
it resides the real endowment of our nature for which we
owe thanks.

How can we give thanks for this endowment, the gift of
being able to think what is most thought-provoking, more
fittingly than by giving thought to the most thought-provoking? The supreme thanks, then, would be thinking? And
the profoundest thanklessness, thoughtlessness? Real
thanks, then, never consists in that we ourselves come bearing gifts, and merely repay gift with gift. Pure thanks is
rather that we simply think—think what is really and
solely given, what is there to be thought.

All thanking belongs first and last in the essential realm
of thinking. But thinking devotes its thought to what is to
be thought, to that which in itself, of its own accord, wants
to be thought about and thus innately demands that we
think back to it. When we think what is most thought-
provoking we think *properly*. When we, in thinking, are
gathered and concentrated on the most thought-provoking,
then we dwell where all recalling thought is gathered.

The gathering of thinking back into what must be
thought is what we call the memory.

We do not understand this word any longer in its common meaning. Instead, we are following the directive of
the ancient word. And we take it by no means only in the
sense of written history. We are heeding what is called by
name in it, and what is unspoken in it, and at the same time
are keeping in view all that has meanwhile been said about
thinking as thanks and as memory and thinking back.

Summary and Transition

What is called thinking? This time we shall take the question in the sense listed first, and ask: What does the word

"thinking" say? Where there is thinking, there are thoughts. By thoughts we understand opinions, ideas, reflections, propositions, notions. But the Old English word "thanc" says more than that—more not only in terms of the usual meaning mentioned here, but something different; and different not only by comparison with what went before, but different in nature, in that it is decidedly distinct and also decisive. The *thanc* means man's inmost mind, the heart, the heart's core, that innermost essence of man which reaches outward most fully and to the outermost limits, and so decisively that, rightly considered, the idea of an inner and an outer world does not arise.

When we listen to the word *thanc* in its basic meaning, we hear at once the essence of the two words: thinking and memory, thinking and thanks, which readily suggest themselves in the verb "to think."

The *thanc*, the heart's core, is the gathering of all that concerns us, all that we care for, all that touches us insofar as we are, as human beings. What touches us in the sense that it defines and determines our nature, what we care for, we might call contiguous or contact. For the moment, the word may strike us as odd. But it grows out of the subject matter it expresses, and has long been spoken. It is only that we fail too easily to hear what is spoken.

Whenever we speak of subject and object, there is in our thoughts a project and a base, an oppositeness—there is always contact in the widest sense. It is possible that the thing which touches us and is in touch with us if we achieve our humanity, need not be represented by us constantly and specifically. But even so it is concentrated, gathered *toward* us beforehand. In a certain manner, though not exclusively, we ourselves are that gathering.

The gathering of what is next to us here never means an after-the-fact collection of what basically exists, but the tidings that overtake all our doings, the tidings of what we are committed to beforehand by being human beings.

Only because we are by nature gathered in contiguity can we remain concentrated on what is at once present and past and to come. The word "memory" originally means this incessant concentration on contiguity. In its original telling sense, memory means as much as devotion. This word possesses the special tone of the pious and piety, and designates the devotion of prayer, only because it denotes the all-comprehensive relation of concentration upon the holy and the gracious. The *thanc* unfolds in memory, which persists as devotion. Memory in this originary sense later loses its name to a restricted denomination, which now signifies no more than the capacity to retain things that are in the past.

But if we understand memory in the light of the old word *thanc*, the connection between memory and thanks will dawn on us at once. For in giving thanks, the heart in thought recalls where it remains gathered and concentrated, because that is where it belongs. This thinking that recalls in memory is the original thanks.

The originary word *thanc* allows us to hear what the word "thinking" tells us. This manner of hearing corresponds to the essential situation which the word *thanc* designates. This manner of hearing is the decisive one. Through it, we understand what "thinking" calls for, by way of the *thanc*. The current familiar usage, by contrast, leads us to believe that thinking does not stem from thought, but that thoughts first arise out of thinking.

However, we must listen still more closely to the sphere that appeals to us in the originary words "*thanc*," "memory," "thanks." What gives us food for thought ever and again is the most thought-provoking. We take the gift it gives by giving thought to what is most thought-provoking.

In doing so, we keep thinking what is most thought-provoking. We recall it in thought. Thus we recall in thought that to which we owe thanks for the endowment of our nature—thinking. As we give thought to what is most thought-provoking, we give thanks.

To the most thought-provoking, we devote our thinking of what is to-be-thought. But this devoted thought is not something that we ourselves produce and bring along, to repay gift with gift. When we think what is most thought-provoking, we then give thought to what this most thought-provoking matter itself gives us to think about. This thinking which recalls, and which *qua* thinking alone is true thanks, does not need to repay, nor be deserved, in order to give thanks. Such thanks is not a recompense; but it remains an offering; and only by this offering do we allow that which properly gives food for thought to remain what it is in its essential nature. Thus we give thanks for our thinking in a sense that is almost lost to our language, and, so far as I can see, is retained only in our Alemannic usage. When the transaction of a matter is settled, or disposed of, we say in Alemannic dialect that it is "thanked." Disposing does not mean here sending off, but the reverse: it means to bring the matter forth and leave it where it belongs. This sort of disposing is called thanking.

If thinking could dispose of that which ever and again gives food for thought, dispose it into its own nature, such thinking would be the highest thanks mortals can give. Such thinking would be the thankful disposal of what is most thought-provoking, into its most integral seclusion, a seclusion where the most thought-provoking is invulnerably preserved in its problematic being. Not one of us here would presume to claim that he is even remotely capable of such thinking, or even a prelude to it. At the very most, we shall succeed in preparing for it.

But assuming that some men will be capable of it some

day, of thinking in the mode of such thankful disposal
then this thinking would at once be concentrated in the
recall which recalls what is forever most thought-provoking. Then thinking would dwell within memory—memory
understood in the sense of its originary expression.

LECTURE
IV

———————

Memory initially signifies man's inner disposition, and devotion. But these words are used here in the widest and most essential sense. "Disposition," man's heart, has a larger meaning than that given to it in modern speech; it means not merely the sensitive and emotive side of human consciousness, but the essential being of all human nature. In Latin it is called *animus*, as distinct from *anima*.

In this distinction, *anima* means the fundamental determinant of every living being, including human beings. Man can be conceived as an organism, and has been so conceived for a long time. Man so conceived is then ranked with plants and animals, regardless of whether we assume that rank order to show an evolution, or classify the genera of organisms in some other way. Even when man is marked out as the rational living being, he is still seen in a way in which his character as an organism remains decisive— though biological phenomena, in the sense of animal and vegetable beings, may be subordinated to that rational and personal character of man which determines his life of the spirit. All anthropology continues to be dominated by the idea that man is an organism. Philosophical anthropology as well as scientific anthropology will *not* use man's essential nature as the starting point for their definition of man.

If we are to think of man not as an organism but a

human being, we must first give attention to the fact that man is that being who has his being by pointing to what is, and that particular beings manifest themselves as such by such pointing. Yet that which is, does not complete and exhaust itself in what is actual and factual at the given moment. To all that is—which is to say, to all that continues to be determined by Being—there belongs just as much, and perhaps even more, what can be, what must be, and what *is* in the past. Man is the being who is in that he points toward "Being," and who can be himself only as he always and everywhere refers himself to what is.

In a way it has never been possible to overlook altogether this characteristic of human nature. We shall soon see where and how philosophy has found a place for this characteristic trait in human nature. However, it still makes a decisive difference whether this trait of the living being "man" is merely included in our considerations as a distinguishing mark superadded to the living being—or whether this relatedness to what is, *because* it is the basic characteristic of man's human nature, is given its decisive role as the *standard*. And this is not done where the fundamental determinant of man's human nature is conceived as *anima*, nor where it is conceived as *animus*. *Animus*, it is true, means that inner striving of human nature which always is determined by, attuned to, what is. The Latin word *animus* can also be translated with the word "soul." "Soul" in this case means not the principle of life, but that in which the spirit has its being, the spirit of the spirit, Master Eckehart's "spark" of the soul. The soul in this sense is what Mörike speaks of in his poem "Think it, my soul." Among contemporary poets, Georg Trakl likes to use the word "soul" in an exalted sense. The third stanza of his poem "The Thunderstorm" begins:

> "O pain, thou flaming vision
> of the great soul!"

What the Latin word *animus* intends is designated more fully in the originary words "memory" and "thanc." Here also is the juncture along our way where we set out to take an even more essential step. That step leads to the sphere where the nature of memory shows itself to us in a more primal manner—not just in terms of the word, but in substance. We do not claim that the nature of memory, as it must now be thought of, is named in the initial, primal word. Rather, the initial meaning of the ancient word gives us a clue. The suggestions that follow up this clue are no more than a groping attempt to render the ground visible on which the nature of memory rests. That attempt is supported by something which has appeared at the beginning of Western thought, and has never quite faded from its horizon.

In what direction does it point, the thing we commented on as the nature of memory? Within the radius of what the originary word "memory" designates, it still looks at first as though memory, in the sense of heart and disposition, were nothing more than a part of man's natural equipment. Thus we take it for something specifically human. And so it is—but not exclusively, nor even primarily.

We defined memory as the gathering of thinking that recalls. As soon as we give thought to this definition, we no longer stop with it or before it. We follow that to which the definition directs us. The gathering of recalling thought is not based on a human capacity, such as the capacity to remember and retain. All thinking that recalls what can be recalled in thought already lives in that gathering which beforehand has in its keeping and keeps hidden all that remains to be thought.

The nature of that which keeps safe and keeps hidden lies in preserving, in conserving. The "keep" originally means the custody, the guard.

Memory, in the sense of human thinking that recalls,

dwells where everything that gives food for thought is kept in safety. We shall call it the "keeping." It harbors and conceals what gives us food for thought. "Keeping" alone *gives* freely what is to-be-thought, what is most thought-provoking, it frees it *as a gift*. But the keeping is not something that is apart from and outside of what is most thought-provoking. The keeping itself is the most thought-provoking thing, itself is its mode of giving—giving itself which ever and always is food for thought. Memory, as the human recall of what must be thought about, consists in the "keeping" of what is most thought-provoking. Keeping is the fundamental nature and essence of memory.

Our attempt to explain memory as no more than a capacity to retain shows that our ideas stop too soon and too restrictively with the immediate data. Memory is not just part of that capacity to think within which it takes place; rather, all thinking, and every appearance of what is to-be-thought, find the open spaces in which they arrive and meet, only where the keeping of what is most thought-provoking takes place. Man only *inhabits* the keeping of what gives him food for thought—he does not create the keeping.

Only that which keeps safely can preserve—preserve what is to-be-thought. The keeping preserves by giving harbor, and also protection from danger. And from what does the keeping preserve what is to-be-thought? From oblivion. However, the keeping is not *compelled* to preserve in this manner. It can permit the oblivion of what is most thought-provoking. What is our evidence? The evidence is that what is most thought-provoking, what long since and forever gives us food for thought, remains in its very origin withdrawn into oblivion.

The question then arises how we can have the least knowledge of what is most thought-provoking. More pressing still is the question : in what does the essential nature of past being and forgetting consist? We are inclined, because we are so accustomed, to see forgetting only as a failure to retain, and to consider this failure a defect. If what is most thought-provoking remains forgotten, it does not appear. It suffers an injury. At least, so it seems.

In fact, the history of Western thought begins, not by thinking what is most thought-provoking, but by letting it remain forgotten. Western thought thus begins with an omission, perhaps even a failure. So it seems, as long as we regard oblivion only as a deficiency, something negative. Besides, we do not get on the right course here if we pass over an essential distinction. The beginning of Western thought is not the same as its origin. The beginning is, rather, the veil that conceals the origin—indeed an unavoidable veil. If that is the situation, then oblivion shows itself in a different light. The origin keeps itself concealed in the beginning.

Yet all these anticipatory remarks which had to be made, about the nature of memory and its relation to the keeping of what is most thought-provoking, about the keeping and forgetfulness, about the beginning and the origin—all these remarks sound strange to us, because we have only just come close to the things and situations in which what we have said finds expression.

But now we need to take only a few more steps along our way, to become aware that situations are expressed in what was said which we find difficult of access for no other reason than their simplicity. At bottom, a specific access is not even needed here, because what must be thought about is somehow close to us in spite of everything. It is just that it is still hidden from our sight by those old-accustomed preconceptions which are so stubborn because they have their own truth.

We tried to explain the question "What is called thinking?" in respect of that mode of asking it which we had listed in first place. What does the word "thinking" signify? It now speaks in the essential context which is evoked by the words *thanc*, recalling thought, thanks, memory.

But the issues mentioned here do not speak directly to us. They remain in what is unspoken and almost forgotten. The explanation of the first question still presents itself to us as if it had merely reminded us of some old, forgotten heirloom of language. But can we in this way call the word back into the spoken language? No! Then why do we try at all to draw attention to what the word states, since we have to concede that the treasures of language cannot be given artificial currency in a usage somehow refurbished?

If that were what we hope and strive for, we would have to take language, too, for no more than an instrument that can be manipulated now one way and now another. But language is not a tool. Language is not this and that, is not also something else besides itself. Language is language. Statements of this kind have the property that they say nothing and yet bind thinking to its subject matter with supreme conclusiveness. The boundlessness with which such sentences can be abused corresponds to the infinity into which they direct the task of thinking.

We concede: what is spoken in the word "thinking," "*thanc*" remains for us in the realm of the unspoken. When we hear talk of "thinking," we do not only fail to think of what the word says but do in fact form altogether different ideas. The meaning of this word "thinking" is not determined by what is spoken and unspoken in its speech. What the word "thinking" calls by name is determined by a different call. Hence we must ask once more "What is called thinking?"—and in this sense: what has been understood since ancient times by "thinking"?

Instruction on what to understand by "thinking" is given by logic. "Logic"—what is that? How does it get that way, that it decides what is to be understood by thinking? Is logic perchance itself the calling that calls on us to think? Or is logic in turn subject to the calling? What is it that calls on us to think?

The first question, "What does the word 'thinking' signify?," has directed us to the second, "What have we understood since ancient times by the word 'thinking'?" But the second question can be raised only within the context of the decisive fourth. We shall be attending to that fourth question as we now attempt to deal with the second. The second question runs: what, according to the so far prevailing doctrine of thinking, do we understand by "thinking"? Why does this doctrine have the title "logic"?

Such questions bring us into the realm of what is familiar, even most familiar. For thinking, this always remains the real danger zone, because the familiar carries an air of harmlessness and ease, which causes us to pass lightly over what really deserves to be questioned.

Some people get stirred up because, after the reference in my inaugural address "What is Metaphysics?" (1929), I keep on raising the question of logic. Those who are here today cannot know, of course, that since my lectures "Logic," given in the summer of 1934, this title "Logic" conceals "the transformation of logic into the question of the *essential nature* of language"—a question that is something else again than philosophy of language.

Those issues, then, that we shall discuss in subsequent lectures, cannot be urged too strongly and too often upon our reflection. Whether we shall let ourselves become involved in that reflection by clearing its path further, each man for his part, or whether we shall pass it over as something presumably done with: that belongs to a decision which only the few can face.

The name "logic" is an abbreviation of the complete title which, in Greek, runs ἐπιστήμη λογική—the understanding that concerns the λόγος. Λόγος is the noun to the verb λέγειν. Logic understands λέγειν in the sense of λέγειν τι κατά τινος, to say something about something. The something about which a statement is made is in such a case what lies beneath it. What lies beneath is called in Greek ὑποκείμενον, in Latin *subiectum*. That about which the λέγειν states something is the subject of the statement; and that which is stated about it is the predicate. The λόγος, as λέγειν τι κατά τινος, is the assertion of something about something. The what-about of every statement is somehow given. It touches upon, is contiguous to the statement. It is part of the contiguity in the widest sense.

Logic, as the doctrine of the λόγος, considers thinking to be the assertion of something about something. According to logic, such speech is the basic characteristic of thinking. In order for such speech to be possible in the first place, the something about which something is said—the subject— and that which is said—the predicate—must be compatible in speech. Incompatible things cannot be made into a unit by a spoken statement: take, for example, "triangle" and "laughter." The sentence "The triangle is laughing" cannot be said. It can be said, of course, in the sense that it can be pronounced as a mere string of words; we just did so. But it can not be said really, in terms of what it says. The things that are evoked by "triangle" and "laughing" introduce something contradictory into their relation. The terms do make a declaration, but contradict each other. They thus make the proposition impossible. To be possible, the proposition must from the start avoid self-contradiction. This is why the law, that contradiction must be avoided, is considered a basic tenet of the proposition. Only because thinking is defined as λόγος, as an utterance, can the statement about contradiction perform its role as a law of thought.

All this has long been known, perhaps too long, so that we no longer allow ourselves to give thought to the definition of thinking as λόγος. To be sure, in the course of the history of Occidental-European thought it was noted that this thinking, born of the λόγος and shaped by logic, does not cover everything and does not suffice in every respect. We did come upon subjects and whole areas of subject matter that demand a different thinking process in order to become accessible to mental perception. But insofar as thinking is originally performed as λόγος, a change of the thinking process can consist only in a transformation of the λόγος. Accordingly, the λέγειν of the λόγος develops into a διαλέγεσθαι.

Logic becomes dialectic. For dialectic, a λόγος in the customary form of a proposition is never unequivocal. The statement "God is the Absolute" may serve as an example. The ambiguity that is here possible is foreshadowed by the difference in stress with which a statement of this kind can be pronounced: *God* is the Absolute—or, God is *the Absolute*. The first sentence means: God alone can claim the distinction of being the Absolute. The second sentence means: only by virtue of the absoluteness of the Absolute is God essentially God. The statement "God is the Absolute" is shown to have several meanings. In appearance, the sentence is a simple proposition, a λόγος in the sense defined.

This is not yet the place to discuss whether the ambiguity of this λόγος is inherent in logic, or whether the logicality of the λόγος, and thus the λόγος itself, has its grounds elsewhere. In any event, propositions such as our "God is the Absolute" do not stay fixed when we say them thoughtfully, that is, when we inquire into what they assert. Their λόγος says only what it is meant to say when it goes through its own λέγειν within and for itself; through is διά; the "for itself" is expressed in λέγεσθαι, the "middle voice" of λέγειν. As διαλέγεσθαι, the λέγειν or proposition proceeds back and forth for itself within its own domain, goes through it, and so covers it to the end. Thought now is dialectical.

We readily see that all dialectic is by its nature logic, whether it develops as the dialectic of consciousness, or as *Realdialektik* and finally dialectical materialism. These, too, must always be a dialectic of objects, which always means objects of consciousness, hence consciousness of self (or one of its germinal forms). In dialectic, too, thinking is defined in terms of the proposition, the λόγος. But where thought encounters things that can no longer be apprehended by logic, those things which are by nature inapprehensible still are within the purview of logic—as a-logical, or no longer logical, or meta-logical (supra-logical).

Summary and Transition

We ask: "What is called thinking?" We ask the question in a fourfold way:

1. What does the word "thinking" signify?
2. What does prevailing doctrine mean by thinking?
3. What is needed for us to accomplish thinking with essential rightness?
4. What is That which calls us into thinking?

These four questions, whose differences we cannot rehearse too often, are nonetheless *one* question. Their unity stems from the question listed in the fourth place. The fourth is the decisive one—it sets the standard. For this fourth question itself asks for the standard by which our nature, as a thinking nature, is to be measured. The third manner of asking is closest to the fourth. The fourth question inquires about That which commands us to think, That which entrusts thinking to us. The third question inquires about us, it asks us what resources we must rally in order to be capable of thinking. The third manner of asking the question has hardly been mentioned so far, and that will not change in what follows. Why? The reason will become clearer if we now consider, in a short excursus, the kind of answer that the question "What is called thinking?" is trying to find. We first see it clearly in the third question. It runs: what is needed, what are the resources we must have, to be capable of thinking with essential rightness? The third question is the most difficult of all to answer, because here it is least possible to supply the answer by giving facts and stating propositions. Even if we were to enumerate various things that belong to essentially right thinking, what is decisive would still remain undecided: to wit, whether everything that belongs to thinking does indeed belong to us because we have already listened to it. Such listening is always up to us alone. We must ourselves discover the one and only way to answer the question "What is called thinking?" in its third form. If we do not find it out, all talk and listening is in vain. And in that case I would urge you to burn your lecture notes, however precise they may be—and the sooner the better.

However, the way in which the third version of the question is answered throws light upon the answering of the other three, because they, including the third question itself, are one single question in virtue of the fourth. Perhaps the question "What is called thinking?" is, as a question, single and unique. For us this means that, when we ask it, we stand at the beginning of a long road whose full extent we can hardly envisage. But our stress on the uniqueness of this question does not mean that we claim credit for the discovery of an important problem. Commonly, an inquiry aims straight for the answer. It rightly looks for the answer alone, and sees to it that the answer is obtained. The answer disposes of the question. By the answer, we rid ourselves of the question.

The question, "What is called thinking?," is of a different kind. When we ask, "What is called bicycle riding?"

we ask for something everybody knows. If there is someone who does not yet know what it calls for, we can teach him— it is a well-known matter. Not so with thinking. It only looks as though we knew what the question really asks. The question itself still remains unasked. The question "What is called thinking?," therefore, does not aim to establish an answer by which the question can be disposed of as quickly and conclusively as possible. On the contrary, one thing and one thing only matters with this question: to make the question problematical.

Even that is a long way off. Indeed it remains questionable whether we are now underway on that way. Perhaps we modern men are still not capable of such a thing. However, this supposition means more than merely an admission of our weakness.

Thinking—more precisely, the attempt and the duty to think—is now approaching an era when the high demands which traditional thinking believed it was meeting, and pretended it had to meet, become untenable. The way of the question "What is called thinking?" lies even now in the shadow of this weakness. The weakness can be described in four statements:

1. Thinking does not bring knowledge as do the sciences.
2. Thinking does not produce usable practical wisdom.
3. Thinking solves no cosmic riddles.
4. Thinking does not endow us directly with the power to act.

As long as we still subject thinking to these four demands, we shall overrate and overtax it. Both excesses prevent us from returning to a no longer customary modesty and to persist in it, amid the bustle of a civilization that clamors daily for a fresh supply of latest novelties, and daily chases after excitement. And yet the way of thinking, the way of the question "What is called thinking?," remains unavoidable as we go into the coming era. We can have no foreknowledge of what that era will hold, but it is possible to give thought to the signs that signal its derivation and its advent.

Thinking is the most precursory of all precursory activities of man in this era, when Europe's modern age is just beginning to spread over the earth and be consummated. Moreover, it is not just a surface matter of nomenclature whether we look on the present age as the end of modern times, or whether we discern that today the perhaps protracted process of the consummation of modern times is *just starting*.

The question "What is called thinking?" is an attempt to reach that unavoidable way which will lead to the most precursory step. Indeed, the question is prior even to thinking, which is itself the most precursory step. Thus it appears to be a question of the kind to which modern philosophy liked to lay claim as it went looking for the most radical question—the question without presuppositions—which was to lay the unshakable foundations of the entire edifice of the system of philosophy for all future ages. But the question "What is called thinking?" is not without presuppositions. Far from it, it is going directly toward what would here be called presupposition, and becomes involved in it.

The decisive sense of the question is expressed when we ask "What is it that calls on us to think?" Which is the call that claims man's thinking? This question, one might say, already presupposes that thinking is by nature something that is called for, and is maintained and, so to speak, retained within its nature only by the call. The question "What is This that calls us into thought?" already presupposes that thinking, *qua* thinking alone, pays heed to the calling within it.

Thinking, then, is here not taken as an occurrence whose course is open to psychological observation. Nor is thinking

conceived merely as an activity that obeys norms and a
scale of values. Thinking can be guided by validity and
authority only if it has in itself a calling, directing it to
what there is to-be-thought. The question "What is This
that calls on us to think?," if asked with sufficient urgency,
brings us also to the problem *that* thinking, *qua* thinking,
is essentially a call.

That something is, and that it is such and such, is what
we usually designate as a fact. "Fact" is a beautiful and
beguiling word. Prevailing thought has long since formed
firm views on what it means. These views have existed
from that moment on when a distinction, long in preparation, came into view—the distinction between *what* something is, τί ἐστιν, and *that* it is, ὅτι ἔστιν. Later terminology
distinguished between *essentia* and *existentia*, essence and
existence. What we are to think of the explanation which
traditional thinking gives of the existence of a fact, is something that can be decided only after we consider *that* distinction *by* which both *existentia* and *essentia* first achieve
their determination. By what authority, and on what
grounds, is that distinction made? How and in what way is
thinking called to this distinction? The remainder of the
problematic nature of that distinction allows us once again
to fathom the implications of the precursory question
"What calls on us to think?," without involving us pre-
maturely now in the mystery, and also fruitfulness, of the
question. The presumption is that *we* can always ask this
question only in a thinking way, and only in that way can
pose the question in its befitting problematic.

The course of lectures has brought us to the second way
in which the question needs to be developed. It runs: what,
in the so far customary and long since implicit sense, do
we understand by thinking? The implicitness betrays itself
in the fact that what we understand by thinking is presented and handed on by a doctrine bearing the title

"logic." The doctrine of thinking bears that title right-fully : for thinking is the λέγειν of the λόγος.

This name here means to affirm, to predicate, something of something : "The moon has risen." To predicate does not mean here primarily to express in speech, but to present something as something, affirm something as something. Such presentation and affirmation is ruled by a conjunction of what is stated with that about which the statement is made. The conjunction is expressed in the "as" and the "about." The conjunction constitutes a sentence. Every proposition is a sentence. But not every sentence is a proposition. "What is called thinking?" is not a proposition, though it is a sentence—to wit, a direct question.

Every proposition is *ipso facto* a sentence. But we need to give thought to the question whether every statement is a proposition—indeed, whether the statement can at all be defined in terms of the sentence, as the grammarians believe.

Is the statement in the first verse of Matthias Claudius' *Even Song*, "The moon has risen," a proposition, or even a sentence? Of what nature is this statement? I do not know. Nor do I trust myself to discuss the matter. To say that the statement "The moon has risen" is part of a poem, and thus is poetry and not thought, does not help us out of our predicament. The perfectly correct remark that Claudius' statement is a verse and not a sentence does not help us much, so long as it remains obscure what it means to say that the poetic statement gathers into a poem. Presumably we shall never properly think out what poetry is, until we have reached far enough with our question : "What is called thinking?" Once more it becomes apparent how much of a precursor this unique question is.

LECTURE
V

When we ask our question "What is called thinking?" in the second manner, it turns out that thinking is defined in terms of the λόγος. The basic character of thinking is constituted by propositions.

When we ask our question "What is called thinking?" in the first manner, then the word "thinking" directs us to the essential sphere of memory, devotion, and thanks. In the two questions, thinking emerges from different sources of its essential nature. One might be tempted to explain the difference offhand in terms of linguistic designation. Among the Greeks, the name for the basic form of thinking, the proposition, is λόγος. Among ourselves, the name for the thing that is also concealed in the λόγος happens to be "thinking." Linguistically, the word is related to thought, memory, and thanks. But this explanation explains nothing so far, assuming any explanation could be fruitful here. The decisive question still remains this: why is it that for Greek thinking, hence Western and especially European thinking (and for us of today), thinking receives its essential character to this day from what in Greek is called λέγειν and λόγος? Just because at one time the calling into thought took place in terms of the λόγος, logistics today is developing into the global system by which all ideas are organized.

And why does the determination of the essence of thought not take place in terms of those things that are evoked in the sphere of these words *thanc,* "memory," "thanks"—particularly since what these words designate was in its essential profundity by no means unknown to the Greeks? The differences in the essential sources of thinking to which we have alluded do not, then, inhere in any way in the distinctive linguistic designations. Rather, the one and only thing that is decisive for what even still for us constitutes the basic character of thinking—the λέγειν of the λόγος, the proposition, the judgment—is that call by which thinking has been called, and is still being called, into its long-habituated nature.

When we raise the second question, what do we understand by thinking according to the prevailing doctrine, it looks at first as though we were merely seeking historical information about what view of the nature of thinking had come to predominate and is still in force. But if we ask the second question *qua* second question, that is, in the unitary context of the four modes of which we spoke, we then ask it ineluctably in the sense of the decisive fourth question. Then the question runs: what is the calling that has directed and is still directing us into thinking in the sense of the predicative λόγος?

This question is no longer historical—in the sense of narrative history—though it is an historic question. But it is not historic in the sense that it represents some occurrence as a chain of events in the course of which various things are brought about—among them this, that thinking after the manner of the λόγος achieved validity and currency. The question: "What call has directed the mode of thinking to the λέγειν of the λόγος?," is an historic, perhaps *the* historic question, though in the sense that it determines our destiny. It asks what it is that destines our nature to think according to the λόγος, that directs it there, and there turns it to use, and thus implies many possible turns. Thus Plato's definition of the nature of thought is not identical with that of Leibniz, though it is the same. They belong together in that both reveal *one* basic nature, which appears in different ways.

But the fateful character of being destined to such thinking, and thus that destiny itself, will never enter our horizon so long as we conceive the historic from the start only as an occurrence, and occurrence as a causal chain of events. Nor will it do to divide the occurrences so conceived into those whose causal chain is transparent and comprehensible, and others that remain incomprehensible and opaque, what we normally call "fate." The call as destiny is so far from being incomprehensible and alien to thinking, that on the contrary it always is precisely what must be thought, and thus is waiting for a thinking that answers to it.

In order to be equal to the question what, by prevailing doctrine, is called "thinking," we simply have to risk *asking* the question. This implies: we must submit, deliver ourselves specifically to the calling that calls on us to think after the manner of the λόγος. As long as we ourselves do not set out from where we are, that is, as long as we do not open ourselves to the call and, with this question, get underway toward the call—just so long we shall remain blind to the mission and destiny of our nature. You cannot talk of colors to the blind. But a still greater ill than blindness is delusion. Delusion believes that it sees, and that it sees in the only possible manner, even while this its belief robs it of sight.

The destiny of our fateful-historic Western nature shows itself in the fact that our sojourn in this world rests upon thinking, even where this sojourn is determined by the Christian faith—faith which cannot be proved by thinking, nor is in need of proof because it is faith.

But this, that we hardly discern the destiny of our nature, and therefore pay no heed to the calling that has called us to thinking according to the λόγος, flows from still another source. The influence of that source is not up to us. But we are not for that reason excused from admitting that our understanding and explaining, our knowledge and our intelligence—that our thinking still remains totally without mission in terms of the destiny of its own being. The more completely our thinking regards itself merely in terms of its own comparative written history, and historical in *this* sense, the more decisively it will petrify in fatelessness, and the less it will arrive at the artless, fateful relation to the calling by which thinking has been directed to the basic character of the λόγος.

Our age rages in a mad, steadily growing craving to conceive history in terms of universal history, as an occurrence. Its frenzy is exacerbated and fed by the quick and easy availability of sources and means of presentation. This sounds like an exaggeration, but is a fact: the unexpressed archetype of the portrayal of all and everything in terms of universal history that is palatable today is the illustrated weekly. Universal history, operating with the most comprehensive means, assumes that a comparative portrayal of the most varied cultures, from ancient China to the Aztecs, can establish a relation to world history. This world history, however, is not the destiny of a world but rather the object established by conceiving world in terms of universal history, thus: the occurrence, to be presented from every angle, of every human achievement and failure that can in any way be found out.

World history, however, is the destiny whereby a world lays claim to us. We shall never hear that claim of the world's destiny while we are engaged on world-historic— which in this context always means universal-historical— voyages. We shall hear it only by giving heed to the simple calling of our essential mission, so that we may give it thought. The most precursory attempt to pay attention to this way is the question "What does call on us to think?" Note that we say : the question.

But even when we ask what the call to think according to the λόγος is—must we not even then go back to the early ages of Western thinking in order to comprehend what call directed this thinking to begin? This, too, seems to be only a narrative-historical and besides very risky question. After all, we know little about the early thinking of the Greeks, and that little only in fragments, and these fragments of disputed meaning. All we have left of the works of the decisive early thinkers can be put in a pamphlet of not more than thirty pages. What does that amount to, compared with the long shelves of voluminous tomes with which the works of later philosophers keep us occupied?

Inevitably it begins to look as though the attempt to ask the question "What is called thinking?" in the second manner also amounts to no more than a historical consideration of the beginnings of Western philosophy. We shall let it go at that, not because we are indifferent to that impression, but because it cannot be dispelled by talking about it instead of setting out on the way of our question.

What is that calling which commends our Western thinking to its own proper beginnings, and from there still directs even today's thinking on its way? The thinkers of the fateful beginnings of Western thought did not, of course, raise the question of the calling, as we are trying to do now. What distinguishes the beginning is rather that those thinkers experienced the claim of the calling by responding to it in thought. But with such a destiny, must they not also have come to comprehend explicitly the calling that starts their thinking on its way? We may assume so, simply because any thinking is sent out on its way only when it is addressed by that which gives food for thought as that which is to-be-thought. In this address, however, the source of the call itself appears, though not in its full radiance nor under the same name. But before inquiring about the calling that encompasses all Western and modern European thinking, we must try to listen to an early saying which gives us evidence how much early thought generally responds to a call, yet without naming it, or giving it thought, as such. Perhaps we need no more than to recall this one testimony in order to give the fitting, that is, a restrained answer to that question of the initial calling.

The doctrine of thinking is called logic because thinking develops in the λέγειν of the λόγος. We are barely capable of comprehending that at one time this was not so, that a calling became "needful" in order to set thinking on the way of the λόγος into the λέγειν. A fragment of Parmenides, which has been given the number 6, begins with these words: χρὴ τὸ λέγειν τε νοεῖν τ᾽ ἐὸν ἔμμεναι." The usual translation of the saying is: "One should both say and think that Being is."

Summary and Transition

The answer to the question "What is called thinking?" is, of course, a statement, but not a proposition that could be formed into a sentence with which the question can be put aside as settled. The answer to the question is, of course, an utterance, but it speaks from a correspondence. It follows the calling, and maintains the question in its problematic. When we follow the calling, we do not free ourselves of what is being asked.

The question cannot be settled, now or ever. If we proceed to the encounter of what is here in question, the calling, the question becomes in fact only more problematical. When we are questioning within this problematic, we are thinking.

Thinking itself is a way. We respond to the way only by

remaining underway. To be underway on the way in order
to clear the way—that is one thing. The other thing is to
take a position somewhere along the road, and there make
conversation about whether, and how, earlier and later
stretches of the way may be different, and in their difference might even be incompatible—incompatible, that is, for
those who never walk the way, nor ever set out on it, but
merely take up a position outside it, there forever to formulate ideas and make talk about the way.

In order to get underway, we do have to set out. This is
meant in a double sense: for one thing, we have to open
ourselves to the emerging prospect and direction of the way
itself; and then, we must get on the way, that is, must take
the steps by which alone the way becomes a way.

The way of thinking cannot be traced from somewhere
to somewhere like a well-worn rut, nor does it at all exist as
such in any place. Only when we walk it, and in no other
fashion, only, that is, by thoughtful questioning, are we on
the move on the way. This movement is what allows the
way to come forward. That the way of thought is of this
nature is part of the precursoriness of thinking, and this
precursoriness in turn depends on an enigmatic solitude,
taking the word "solitude" in a high, unsentimental sense.

No thinker ever has entered into another thinker's solitude. Yet it is only from its solitude that all thinking, in a
hidden mode, speaks to the thinking that comes after or that
went before. The things which we conceive and assert to be
the results of thinking, are the misunderstandings to which
thinking ineluctably falls victim. Only they achieve publication as alleged thought, and occupy those who do *not*
think.

To answer the question "What is called thinking?" is
itself always to keep asking, so as to remain underway. This
would seem easier than the intention to take a firm position; for adventurer-like, we roam away into the unknown.

Nevertheless, if we are to remain underway we must first of all and constantly give attention to the way. The movement, step by step, is what is essential here. Thinking clears its way only by its own questioning advance. But this clearing of the way is curious. The way that is cleared does not remain behind, but is built into the next step, and is projected forward from it.

Now it always remains possible, of course, and very often actually is the case, that we dislike a way of this sort from the start, because we consider it hopeless or superfluous, or because we consider it foolishness. If that is our attitude, we should refrain from looking at the way even from outside. But perhaps it is not fitting anyhow to let the way be seen in public. With this hint, we shall break off our general remarks about ways of thinking.

We shall now try to walk the way of our question, by asking it in the sense of the decisive fourth, but in the mode of the second manner.

The initially proposed version of the second question ran: what do we understand by thinking according to traditional doctrine, logic? At first it appears that the question inquires historically what we have hitherto had in mind and taught about thinking. But now we ask:

"What is the call to which Western-European thinking is subject, the thinking whose roads we, too, follow as soon as we let ourselves get involved in thinking?"

But even so, the impression unavoidably remains that the question amounts to no more than a historical description of the beginnings of Western philosophy. The treatment of the question may retain this peculiarity, that it will remain forever implausible to the scholarly research in the history of philosophy and its principles of interpretation.

In the writings of Parmenides, a Greek thinker who lived around the turn of the sixth into the fifth century B.C., we read the saying:

"χρὴ τὸ λέγειν τε νοεῖν τ' ἐὸν ἔμμεναι."

According to the usual translations, this means:

"One should both say and think that Being is."

It would be most in keeping with the way on which we have set out with our question, if we were now to leave off all asides and warnings, and tried to trace in thought what the saying tells us. But today, when we know much too much and form opinions much too quickly, when we compute and pigeonhole everything in a flash—today there is no room at all left for the hope that the presentation of a matter might in itself be powerful enough to set in motion any fellow-thinking which, prompted by the showing of the matter, would join us on our way. We therefore need these bothersome detours and crutches that otherwise run counter to the style of thinking ways. This is the necessity to which we bow when we now attempt, by circumscribing the matter in ever narrower circles, to render possible the leap into what the saying tells us:

"χρὴ τὸ λέγειν τε νοεῖν τ' ἐὸν ἔμμεναι."

"One should both say and think that Being is."

LECTURE
VI

One is tempted to call this proposition an obvious platitude. What else can we say and think of being, except that it is? The statement is not only self-evident—it remains totally vacuous. It actually tells us nothing: and what it does tell, we knew before. "Being is" sounds like rain rains. Of course rain rains. What else could it do? And a thinker of Parmenides' stature is supposed to have uttered vacuities of this kind? Still worse, he is even supposed to have offered this vacuity as something it is necessary to say and think?

Let us just suppose that Parmenides did utter the sentence, "being is," and did intend it in the sense we mentioned. Is it as vacuous, as easy to recite, as it would seem? The phrase is not so vacuous as to say the identical thing twice with equal thoughtlessness. Even considered superficially, the phrase proves ambiguous. It may say: being is, meaning it is not so that being is not. What is stated is the actuality of being. But the phrase may also say: part of the fundamental character of being is that "it is": Being. The "what" of being, its essence, is named in the "is." Or, the phrase may state both things at once—the fact *that* being is, and *what* it is, its essential nature. Parmenides, it is true, speaks neither of the "existence" nor of the "essence" of being.

To keep us from judging the phrase too lightly, let us try to clarify it by an example. We admit that in this case the procedure remains quite dubious. There is a tree in the yard. We state: the tree is well-shaped. It is an apple tree. This year it did not bear many apples. The birds like it. The apple-grower has still other things to say about it. The scientific botanist, who conceives of the tree as a plant, can point out a variety of things about the tree. And finally there comes along a strange and curious human being and says: the tree is, it is not so that the tree is not.

Now, which is easier to say and to think—all those things that have been reported about the tree from the most diverse quarters, or the phrase: "The tree is!"? If we say this phrase and if, in the saying, it is a λέγειν, a thinking and not just vapid talk—then, I ask again: what about the tree is easier to determine, its lovely shape and all the other things that can be perceived—or this, that the tree is?

If we stop only for one moment to say the phrase: "The tree is," saying it in terms of what the phrase says, we have already said "is" about the tree. And now *we* are faced with the question, clumsy but definite: what about this "is," according to which it is not so that the tree is not? Where in the tree or on the tree or behind the tree, is this thing named by the "is"? We say "is" hundreds of times daily, of course. And even if we do not say it, we constantly and everywhere refer with the auxiliary verb to that which is. But can this fact alone, that we take the "is" so lightly, constitute any kind of evidence that the word itself has no gravity? Who would have the temerity to deny roundly and on no particular grounds that ultimately this auxiliary verb may even name the gravest and most difficult thing that remains to be said?

Let us for the moment strike out the "is," and the phrase "the tree is." Let us assume it had not yet been said. And now let us try to say: the tree is well-shaped; the tree is an apple tree; the tree does not yield many apples. Without the "is" in the phrase "the tree is," these statements would fall into a void, taking along with them the whole science of botany. Nor is that all. Every human attitude to something, every human stand in this or that sphere of beings, would rush away resistlessly into the void if the "is" did not *speak*. Without it, human nature could not even rush *away* into the void, because for the "away" there must have been a "here."

We note once more: the fact that we take the "is" too lightly is no proof that the "is" and what it names does not keep within it a weightiness that we can hardly ever weigh. But that we can take this "is" so lightly shows how much we still are in the constant danger of illusion—an illusion all the more deceptive because it does not appear even to exist.

Yet it would be rash to derogate the appearance of that danger's non-existence as if it were something defective and baneful. That appearance, and the apparent indifference of the "is" that goes with it, may hold the only possibility for mortal men to reach the truth.

The phrase "being is" keeps an infinite distance from empty platitudes. On the contrary, it holds the most completely fulfilled secret of all thinking, in the first intimation of its statement.

And still the question remains open whether the saying of Parmenides demands no more than that we note the fact that being is. This is what we assumed at first, on the strength of the familiar translation. But every translation is already an interpretation. Every interpretation must first of all have entered into what is said, into the subject matter it expresses. Such entering is in our case presumably not as easy as entering an orchard and there to speak of a tree. To enter into what is said in the phrase "being is" remains uncommonly difficult and troublesome for the reason that we are already within it.

But before we enter into the saying of Parmenides we have quoted, we must note that the saying is not offered by Parmenides as the expression of a demand *he* makes. Rather, the saying is addressed to Parmenides himself. For there soon follow the words:

"*τά σ' ἐγὼ φράζεσθαι ἄνωγα*"
"This, the *χρὴ τὸ λέγειν* and other things, I call upon you to take to heart."

Ἐγώ, "I." Who is this "I"? It is in any case a being who calls, in any case a call which speaks to the thinking thinker, and even speaks to him of ways. It shows to him three ways: one which thinking must go before all other ways; one to which thinking must also pay heed as it proceeds; and one which remains impassable to thinking. The calling calls thinking to the crossroads of way, no way, and wrong way. But the way of thinking is of such a kind that this crossroads can never be crossed by a once-for-all decision and choice of way, and the way can never be put behind as once-for-all behind us. The crossroads accompanies us on the way, every moment. Where does this strange triple way lead? Where else but into what is always problematical, always worthy of questioning?

By the words of Parmenides it can be shown that he is subject to a call, that he recounts what is addressed to him in order to respond to it. But we prefer to give our attention directly to what is recounted here, and in and through it raise the question what it is that is addressed to him, rather than prove from the outside, and at length, and fundamentally in vain, that what speaks here is something like a calling.

Let us listen to the thinker's words:

"*χρὴ τὸ λέγειν τε νοεῖν τ' ἐὸν ἔμμεναι*"

But how are we to hear without translating, translate without interpreting? Even if we were dealing with something a thinker said in our native language, it would have to be interpreted. We give attention to the saying while we are underway on the way of the question "What calls on us to think?," in the sense of the λόγος whose laws and nature are expressed in logic. But then, would we not be forcing Parmenides' saying from the start into a specific perspective that is solely determined by the prospect opened up by the way of our question? That is indeed the case. But it is not a defect which we admit only under stress. At most, we here encounter the same difficulty with which every interpretation has to struggle.

But it becomes necessary here to point out an illusion to which we all too easily fall victim again and again. It is that we imagine we are approaching Parmenides' saying in an objective manner and without presuppositions when we take cognizance of it without any intimations and even without giving it thought. We take cognizance of it, we add it to the knowledge which we imagine we possess anyway of such matters. But this "cognizance-taking" without intimations and questions, and seemingly not burdened with any prejudice, is in fact an interpretation as charged with presuppositions and prejudices as is possible in this case. It rests on the stubborn and widespread prior assumption that one can enter into dialogue with a thinker by addressing him out of thoughtlessness. And here thoughtlessness is to be found not so much where someone untrained in philosophy asks his questions, but rather where every seemingly pertinent and apposite citation from all of the world's philosophical literature is indiscriminately thrown in.

But in what way are we to translate the saying? Only *one* way is open. Without regard to later philosophy and its achievements in interpreting this thinker, we shall try to listen to the saying, so to speak, in the first bloom of the words. We must be guided, of course, by a certain familiarity with all that has come down to us of Parmenides' sayings. This will remain in the background of the discussion to follow.

But we shall keep the current translation in view, for the sake of contrast with the translation that we shall now attempt, and not in the conviction that we have thus fully confronted prevailing Parmenides interpretations. A full confrontation could not be satisfied with weighing the results of the various interpretations against each other. That would mean to neglect the main issue. Full confrontation consists in the critical analysis of the unspoken assumptions of prevailing Parmenides interpretations, for which this is not the occasion.

Every confrontation of two different interpretations of a work, not only in philosophy, is in reality a mutual reflection on the guiding presuppositions; it is the discussion of these presuppositions—a task which, strangely, is always tolerated only marginally and covered up with empty generalities. In noting this fact, let us also point out once more that the attempt at translation here proposed—it too, and it most of all—is possible only on the way on which we are already engaged when we ask the question: "What calls on us to think?" With this, the prior assumption of our interpretation is both identified and submitted for discussion.

But it would violate the meaning of interpretation generally if we cherished the view that there can be an interpretation which is non-relative, that is, absolutely valid. Absolutely valid can at the very most be only the sphere of ideas within which we beforehand place the text to be interpreted. And the validity of the presupposed sphere of ideas can be absolute only if the absoluteness rests on something unconditional—on a faith.

The unconditional character of faith, and the problematic character of thinking, are two spheres separated by an abyss.

Every interpretation is a dialogue with the work, and with the saying. However, every dialogue becomes halting and fruitless if it confines itself obdurately to nothing but what is directly said—rather than that the speakers in the dialogue involve each other in *that* realm and abode about which they are speaking, and lead each other to it. Such involvement is the soul of dialogue. It leads the speakers into the unspoken. The term "conversation" does, of course, express the fact that the speakers are turning to one another. Every conversation is a kind of dialogue. But true dialogue is never a conversation. Conversation consists in slithering along the edges of the subject matter, precisely without getting involved in the unspoken. Most textual interpretations—not only of philosophical texts—remain at the level of a conversation, which may often be rich and informative. And that, in many cases, is enough.

In our case it is not enough. We are posing a question. We are asking for the unspoken call that points to the beginnings of Western thinking, the beginning whose course we, too, today still follow in our thinking, though Western is for the moment submerged in European thinking:

"χρὴ τὸ λέγειν τε νοεῖν τ' ἐὸν ἔμμεναι"

"One should both say and think that Being is."

Summary and Transition

Now we must translate Parmenides' saying. What matters here is only the translation—we are still far from a formal interpretation. But even the translation must be careful in two respects. The first concerns the content of the saying. The second concerns the manner in which we carry it over from the Greek into our own language.

1. *The content of the saying*. It all too easily escapes us and slips away into obviousness. It hardly offers enough

purchase to our accustomed ideas to detain us. It offers us no food for thought. Why are we in danger of being done so quickly with a sentence such as "being is"? For one thing, because when we hear the sentence we find nothing in it worthy of thought. We take the view that subject and predicate of the sentence are equally clear: being—is there anyone who does not know being? And "is"—who cares, considering we already have our hands full with *what* is, which also includes after all everything that has been and is coming; everything that is no more and is not yet and thus *is* in some way, always. We have done with this "is," even before it is spoken. And not only we.

The danger of having done with things in this frivolous way has another and primary reason: that in the course of two and a half thousand years, thinking itself has slowly become accustomed to the idea which the sentence states. Hence the theory could arise that nothing further could be said about what the "is" tells us. Kant himself counts the words "being" and "existence" among the "almost un-analysable concepts." He speaks about it in a short, still underestimated work which dates from 1763 (eighteen years before his principal work, *Critique of Pure Reason*) and is entitled *The Only Possible Proof for a Demonstration of the Existence of God* (*Der einzig moegliche Beweisgrund zu einer Demonstration des Daseins Gottes*). Kant's judgment, that "being" belongs among the "almost unanalysable concepts," is indeed fully justified once we share his assumption that what the words "being" and "existence" designate can be grasped primarily and only in a concept.

No wonder then that we no longer notice at all the unheard-of sense of this sentence "being is," much less are touched by it to the point where our entire nature is so shaken that it will never again be the same. Through the centuries this sentence, in many vagrant variations and in many ways has, explicitly or tacitly, been and remained the leading theme of thinking.

Today, when talk about "being" and "existence" is practically a daily routine, we notice only the monotony of the sentence "being is." At best, we are offended by the elusiveness of the apparent generality and abstraction it expresses. Indeed, the most emphatic reminder that what the sentence says in truth is something altogether different, can for the present have hardly any effect.

And yet the day may come when someone will find the sentence astonishing nonetheless, and will notice that all the centuries that have passed away have not been able to diminish it—that unbeknownst to us it has remained as problematical as ever. This is why the sentence still concerns us at this hour, as directly as it ever did, with one difference only.

Formerly, a radiance all its own illumined what this sentence had to say, so that its problematic vanished in that light. In consequence of a strange darkening, which has nothing to do with a decline and fall of the West, that light later fails to appear. What the sentence says turns into the obvious: "being is." What else can being do than "be," once it is at all? Today we want to know only *why* being is. And so we ask: by what is being caused? Being, after all, is the actual, and as such made actual and active, and is everywhere referred to causes. And in such formulations of our questions we include as obvious that "being" means as much as "actuality."

2. *The translation of the saying.* The sentence "being is" seems to occur in the translation. For this reason alone the translation must meet unusual conditions. Since today's thinking still follows directly in the footsteps of this saying —even when it imagines that it need pay no attention to it—the translation is at no time purely a problem of the historical interpretation of an ancient text about which

philologists disagree. In the case here before us, we shall attempt the translation along the way of the one question: "What calls on us to think?"

The translation is of a special kind, because the saying in translation does more than convey knowledge of an earlier view of philosophy. But at the same time, the translation is nothing special, nothing worthy of distinction; for it stays within the problematic of the question that guides it. The explication of the saying remains within the mandate of translation.

LECTURE
VII

The saying becomes clearer if we take the liberty of inserting three colons, to give a sharper articulation to its word structure. We shall also write the saying in four separate lines:

"χρὴ :
τὸ λέγειν τε νοεῖν τ’ :
ἐὸν :
ἔμμεναι."

Following the usual translation, fitted more closely now to the Greek text, the saying then runs:

"Needful: the saying also thinking too: being: to be."

This arrangement does not make the content of the saying any clearer. Nor is there any need for greater clarity at this time. Every man endowed with understanding understands what is being said here. What we may not understand is only this, that such a saying should occur at all in the works of a thinker. And right away we catch ourselves in the act of slipping past this thing we cannot understand.

How would it be if we took this occasion to be astonished that seemingly so obvious a saying is pronounced with such emphasis in a thinker's works? How would it be if we were

182

astonished about it, and let our astonishment make us aware that perhaps something problematical, something worthy of questioning, is involved here?

We just now stressed the structure of the saying, only in order to get closer to the area of its problematic. The colons we inserted give a first, outward sign of the manner in which the words are put in order relative to one another. The Greek word for order and placement is τάξις. In our saying, the words follow upon each other without connection. They are lined up side by side; "beside," or more exactly "by," is παρά in Greek. The word order of our saying is paratactic and not, as the usual translation represents it: "One should *both* say . . . *that.*" By this "both" and "that," the words are put in a specific order. The connection coordinates them, puts them together in an order; in Greek, "together" is σύν. We speak of "synthesis." The usual translation of the saying puts the words together in an order, by inserting connecting words. In regard to its word order, the translation is syntactic.

Syntax is the study of sentence structure in the widest sense. Our ideas of the structure of languages are formed in terms of syntax. Where we encounter languages that have no syntax, we normally understand their structure to be a deviation from, or a failure to attain, syntactic structure. Paratactic structure is found especially in the languages of primitive peoples. Paratactic speech occurs also in syntactically structured languages, for instance among children. Then everything fits, since children, too, are considered primitive. A child might say about a passing dog: "Bow-wow, bad, bite." Χρὴ τὸ λέγειν τε νοεῖν τ᾽ ἐὸν ἔμμεναι sounds that way.

The fact that an expression of early thinking speaks paratactically fits in splendidly with the common picture we have of those thinkers among whom Parmenides belongs. He is counted among the pre-Socratics or pre-Platonists. This is not just a chronological designation but a downgrading. For Plato is considered the greatest thinker, not only among the Greeks, but of the entire West. Why? Not because his thoughts have ever been established as the greatest in terms of what the task of thinking is. I would not know how that could ever have been done by any thinker. Nor would I know by what yardstick we could ever appraise any thinking as *the* greatest. As great—quite possibly. But thinking so far has presumably not even raised the question in what the peculiar greatness of Plato's thought consists—assuming the greatness of any given thinking lies in the wealth of its problematic.

Plato is considered the West's greatest thinker because Platonism—that is, those things which we subsequently adopted and adapted out of Plato's thinking and along with it—has undeniably exercised the most powerful influence on Western thinking. But are we really satisfied that the greatness of any thinking can be computed from the length and breadth of its effects, and assessed by the volume of assent it has gained? And if effect and influence are to be our yardsticks, then what would Plato, and with him Socrates, be without Parmenides?

Plato himself has kept his origins in mind and memory far more essentially than did the Platonism that came after him. The masters always have an indelible and therefore deeper knowledge of their roots than their disciples can ever achieve.

But to this day, Platonism is struck with naked terror if it is expected to consider what lies behind this philosophy of Plato, which it interprets and posits as the only binding philosophy. If we do consider it, we can do it only in this way: we say that early thinking is not yet as advanced as Plato's. To present Parmenides as a pre-Socratic is even more foolish than to call Kant a pre-Hegelian.

But equally mistaken is the reverse procedure into which

we are easily drawn by any emphatic mention of thinkers such as Parmenides. We then adopt the view that the early thinkers, being first in point of time, are first and foremost in every respect—for which reason it is then deemed advisable to philosophize only in this pre-Socratic manner, and to pronounce all the rest a misunderstanding, a retrogression. Such childish ideas are actually in circulation today. We mention them only in view of the way which we are trying to take.

When we take this way, we come to the point where we, in thought and inquiry, retrace the questioning of a thinker by starting from his own thinking and from nowhere else. This task differs in every respect from the frequently heard demand that we must understand a thinker in his own terms. That is impossible, because no thinker—and no poet —understands himself. How then could anybody else dare claim to understand a thinker—even to understand him better?

The wish to understand a thinker in his own terms is something else entirely than the attempt to take up a thinker's quest and to pursue it to the core of his thought's problematic. The first is and remains impossible. The second is rare, and of all things the most difficult. We shall not be allowed to forget this difficulty for a single moment, in any of the lectures to follow. To speak of an "attempt at thinking" is not an empty phrase meant to simulate humility. The term makes the claim that we are here taking a way of *questioning*, on which the problematic alone is accepted as the unique habitat and *locus* of thinking.

But in view of the rashness of our public, let us note also something else. It may easily happen that soon—even tomorrow—the slogan is promulgated: "Everything depends on the problematic!" That cry seems to identify the crier as one of those who are inquirers. Today every statement either becomes stale and irrelevant at once, or else stays caught in an insidious ambiguity against which the individual is helpless.

"χρὴ τὸ λέγειν τε νοεῖν τ' ἐὸν ἔμμεναι"

We speak and hear the saying paratactically, but still in the usual translation:

"Needful: the saying also thinking too: being: to be."

But we certainly do not take paratactic to mean not-yet syntactic. Nor do we rank it as primitive. We keep it clear of any comparison with the speech of children and of primitive peoples. We also leave the question open whether, when a child says nothing but "moon" at the sight of the moon, or responds to the sight of the moon with a word he has made up himself—whether there is not at work here, for a short moment, a speech far more primary than in the most exquisitely wrought sentence of the man of letters. Is this a reason to elevate the speech and art of children to the principle of a new form of speech, and a new art form? No. Such propositions stem from abstract considerations, and are the exact counterpart of the fabrications of the age of technology, which are something else again than the *essence* of technology.

We call the word order of the saying paratactic in the widest sense simply because we do not know what else to do. For the saying *speaks* where there are no words, in the field between the words which the colons indicate.

Parmenides' language is the language of a thinking; it is that thinking itself. Therefore, it also speaks differently from the still older poetry of Homer.

We shall now follow Parmenides' saying word for word, without taking the view that it is merely a sequence of words.

Χρή comes from the verb χράω, χρῆσθαι. The word derives from ἡ χείρ, the hand; χράω, χράομαι means: I handle and so keep in hand, I use, I have use for. Starting with this use that is practiced by man, we shall try to point out the *nature* of using. It is not anything that man first produces and performs. "Using" does not mean the mere utilizing, using up, exploiting. Utilization is only the degenerate and debauched form of use. When we handle a thing, for example, our hand must fit itself to the thing. Use implies fitting response. Proper use does not debase what is being used—on the contrary, use is determined and defined by leaving the used thing in its essential nature. But leaving it that way does not mean carelessness, much less neglect. On the contrary : only proper use brings the thing to its essential nature and keeps it there. So understood, use itself is the summons which demands that a thing be admitted to its own essence and nature, and that the use keep to it. To use something is to let it enter into its essential nature, to keep it safe in its essence.

Proper use is neither a mere utilizing, nor a mere needing. What we merely need, we utilize from the necessity of a need. Utilizing and needing always fall short of proper use. Proper use is rarely manifest, and in general is not the business of mortals. Mortals are at best illumined by the radiance of use. The essential nature of use can thus never be adequately clarified by merely contrasting it with utilization and need. We speak of usage and custom, of what we are used to. Even such usage is never of its own making. It hails from elsewhere, and presumably is used in the proper sense.

Now, when this word, in the form χρή, is mentioned at the outset of a thoughtful saying, and this particular saying, we may assume without fear of being arbitrary that the "using" mentioned here is spoken in a high, perhaps the highest, sense. We therefore translate χρή with "It is useful . . ." The translation directs us to give thought to something that not only is not customary to our ways of

forming ideas, but that must for the moment remain altogether unthought.

"It is useful." That sounds like "it is raining, it is windy,
it is dawning." Grammar and logic call such sentences impersonal, subjectless sentences. Χρή, then, would be a sentence without a subject. The Latin *pluit*, it is raining, is
of that kind. Raining refers to no person. Accordingly, the
sentence is impersonal. Or does rain rain the same way
thunder thunders? Or does even this statement miss the
mark? We are groping in the dark.

The term "impersonal, subjectless sentences" determines
only something negative, and even that perhaps inadequately. For in sentences of this type, there is always the
"it." Of course, one never ought to talk about the "it" so
long as the essential realm has not been brought into view
to which the word appeals. "It," we explain, means the
impersonal. "It" means something neither masculine nor
feminine. "It" means neither of the two, but the neuter.
Of course.

But since when has it been established that the personal,
and the difference of the genders, are all we need in order
to think the "it" properly—and that means to maintain it
in its problematic—simply by contrasting "it" negatively
with the personal and the genders? The fact that such statements as "it is windy, it is snowing, it is thawing, it is
dawning" and so on, speak with special urgency and fre-
quency of the weather, is something to think about. We
must understand "weather" here in the widest sense, of
atmospheric conditions and storms that show on the face of
the sky. Nobody would claim that grammar and logic have
adequately elucidated the nature of these curious sentences
—"adequately" here meaning also with the necessary re-
serve. Nor would it seem to be their business.

"It is useful." Who or what is "It," we ask; and our
question comes too soon and is too crude. For once again,

without cause and without scruple, we accept it as an established fact that one can and may ask about this "It" exclusively in terms of what, "It"?, or who, "It"? Of course, "it
is useful" does not speak of a phenomenon in the sky, like
"it is raining." As translation of the χρή, the phrase "it is
useful" belongs rather in the company of "there is." This
frequent turn of phrase was mentioned when we tried to
characterize what gives food for thought before all else—
what is most thought-provoking. It gives us food for
thought. (On "there is," compare *Being and Time*, last
part of par. 43 and the beginning of par. 44. Also *Letter on
Humanism*, p. 22.)

Could it be that only the "it is useful"—thought through
generously and adequately—would define more closely
what "there is" says?

Could it be that only when we have extended our quest,
inquired adequately into use and usage—that only then
the "it" in "it is useful" would achieve its radiant appearance?

We therefore point once more to the high sense of *use*
as we here say it. What it tells us becomes clearer only in
the context of the complete saying which speaks in the sense
of χρή. Even so, a more informal reflection on "it is useful"
may bring us closer to the matter.

"It is useful . . ." means something more essential than
"it is needful." For Parmenides' saying is not concerned
with a need in the usual sense, nor with a brute necessity,
and least of all with blind compulsion. The phrase "it is
useful" could evoke such meanings. But even then we must
first ask in every case where that assonance stems from, and
whether it does not give voice to an "it is useful" thought
in a deeper sense. Such is the case with Hoelderlin. We shall
cite two passages from his poetry. But the remarks which
follow do not mean to suggest that Hoelderlin says the same
thing as does χρή, as though Parmenides' thinking could

be interpreted by being traced back to passages from Hoelderlin's poetry.

In the last stanza of his hymn "The Ister River," Hoelderlin says:

> "It is useful for the rock to have shafts,
>   And for the earth, furrows,
>   It would be without welcome, without stay."

There is no welcome where no meal, no food and drink can be offered. There is no stay here for mortals, in the sense of dwelling at home. If mortals are to be made welcome and to stay, there must be water from the rock, wheat from the field:

> "It is useful for the rock to have shafts,
>   And for the earth, furrows."

Shafts pierce the rock. They break a path for the waters. The Greek word for pierce is κεντεῖν; κέντρον is the spike. The centaurs owe their nature to the piercing spear. This piercing and path-breaking is part of "what gives life." Hoelderlin, too, sees it in this light, as one of his enigmatic translations of Pindar fragments (Hell. V, 2, 272) clearly shows. There it says: "The idea of centaurs may well be the idea of the spirit of a stream, since the stream makes a path and a border, by force, on the earth that originally is pathless and growing upward. Its image is therefore in the place of nature where the bank is rich in rocks and grottoes. . . ."

"It is useful for the rock to have shafts/ And for the earth, furrows." We should be listening altogether too superficially, and thinking too little, if we were to interpret the "it is useful" here to mean only "it is necessary . . ." Shafts are no more necessary to the rock than furrows to the earth. But it belongs to the essence of welcome and being at home that it include the welling of water and the fruits of the field. "It is useful" says here: there is an essential community between rock and shaft, between furrow and earth, *within* that realm of being which opens up when the earth becomes a habitation. The home and dwelling of mortals has its own natural site. But its situation is not determined first by the pathless places on earth. It is marked out and opened by something of another order. From there, the dwelling of mortals receives its measure.

Summary and Transition

The key word in Parmenides' saying is χρή. We now translate it with "it is useful." Even on superficial examination the saying speaks of stating and of thinking, of being, of Being. It speaks of the highest and the deepest, the most remote and the nearest, the most veiled and the most apparent that mortal tale can tell. This gives us the occasion and the right to assume that the word χρή, too, is spoken in the highest sense.

"To use" means, first, to let a thing be what it is and how it is. To let it be this way requires that the used thing be cared for in its essential nature—we do so by responding to the demands which the used thing makes manifest in the given instance. Once we understand "using" in this sense, which is more natural to us, and in which using designates a human activity, we have already differentiated it from other modes of acting with which it is easily and readily confused and mixed up: from utilizing, and from needing. In common usage, however, χρή may mean those things as well.

A wide range of meaning belongs generally to the nature of every word. This fact, again, arises from the mystery of language. Language admits of two things: One, that it be reduced to a mere system of signs, uniformly available to everybody, and in this form be enforced as binding; and two, that language at one great moment says one unique thing, for one time only, which remains inexhaustible because it is always originary, and thus beyond the reach of any kind of leveling. These two possibilities of language are so far removed from each other that we should not be doing justice to their disparity even if we were to call them extreme opposites.

Customary speech vacillates between these two possible ways in which language speaks. It gets caught halfway. Mediocrity becomes the rule. Commonness, which looks much like custom, attaches itself to the rule. Common speech puffs itself up as the sole binding rule for everything we say—and now every word at variance with it immediately looks like an arbitrary violation. The translation of the word χρή, likewise, appears arbitrary if instead of saying "One should" we say "It is useful . . ."

But the time may finally have come to release language from the leash of common speech and allow it to remain attuned to the keynote of the lofty statement it makes—without, however, rating customary speech as a decline, or as low. It will then no longer suffice to speak of a lofty statement, for this, too, is, at least in name, still rated by low standards.

Why this reference to language? In order to stress once again that we are moving within language, which means moving on shifting ground or, still better, on the billowing waters of an ocean.

Χρή: "It is useful . . ." Thought in its high signification, that means: to admit into essential nature, and there to keep safely what has been admitted. To attune our ear to this meaning of the word, we shall try to clarify "it is useful" by means of two passages from Hoelderlin's poetry.

One passage is from the hymn "The Ister River":

> "It is useful for the rock to have shafts,
> And for the earth, furrows,
> It would be without welcome, without stay."

In this passage, the "useful" designates an essential community of rock and shaft, earth and furrow. This essential community is in turn determined by the nature of welcome and stay. The welcoming, and the staying, are what marks the dwelling of mortals on this earth. But dwelling, in its turn, is not grounded within itself.

LECTURE
VIII

The other passage of Hoelderlin's poetry is found in the hymn "The Titans":

> "For under the firm measure,
> The crude, too, is useful,
> That the pure may know itself."

"Under the firm measure" means for Hoelderlin "under the sky." According to the late poem that begins "There blooms in lovely blueness . . . ," the face of the sky is the place where the unknown God conceals himself. "Under the firmament," under the sky so conceived, there is the site where mortals inhabit the earth. On earth itself there is no firmament, no firm measure. It cannot be derived from the earth, especially since the earth can never by itself be habitable earth.

> ". . . under the firm measure,
> The crude, too, is useful."

The crude is not an addition to the pure. Nor does the pure have need of the crude. But the crude must be there in order that the pure may become manifest to itself as the pure and thus as that which is other, and thus may have its own being. "Under the firm measure," on the earth under the

194

sky, the pure itself can be the pure only as it admits the crude close to its own essence and there holds it. This does not affirm the crude. Yet the crude exists by rights, because it is being so used with essential rightness.

All this makes difficult thinking. A mere dialectic, with its Yes and No, can never grasp it. Besides, possible misinterpretations threaten on all sides. For neither are we dealing here with a gross justification of the crude, taken by itself, nor does the crude appear merely in the role of a catalyst to bring forth purity, by itself. For, "under the firm measure" there exists neither the splendid self-sovereignty of the pure, nor the self-willed power of the crude, each cut off from its counterpart which it uses.

Once more, the "It is useful . . ." signifies an admittance into the essence, by which the habitation on earth is granted and assured to mortals, that is, kept in safety for them. And a still deeper nature of "using" is concealed in the eighth stanza of the hymn "The Rhine." We are still unprepared to think it through.

In translating χρή in Parmenides' saying with "it is useful," we respond to a meaning of χρή that echoes in the root word. Χράομαι means turning something to use by handling it—which has always been a turning to the thing in hand according to its nature, thus letting that nature become manifest by the handling.

But thinking can so far have only a vague intimation of that high meaning of χρή, "it is useful," which speaks in Parmenides' saying. The "it is useful" which must here be thought, and which Parmenides nowhere elucidates, conceals a still deeper and wider sense than the word does in Hoelderlin's language. Perhaps we shall be able to hear Hoelderlin's language properly only when we comprehend the "it is useful" that is beginning to sound in the χρή of Parmenides' saying.

The user lets the used thing enter into the property of its

own nature, and there preserves it. This admitting and preserving is what distinguishes the using of which we are speaking here, but in no way exhausts its nature. Using, thought of in this way, is no longer, is never the effect of man's doing. But conversely, all mortal doing belongs within the realm in which the χρή makes its appeal. Using commends the used thing to its own nature and essence. In this using there is concealed a command, a calling. In the χρή of Parmenides' saying, a call is identified, although it is not thought out, much less explicated. Every primal and proper identification states something unspoken, and states it so that it remains unspoken.

"χρή : τὸ λέγειν τε νοεῖν τε"
"It is useful : the stating so thinking too . . ."

The Greek verbs λέγειν and νοεῖν, according to the dictionary, are here translated correctly. The dictionary informs us that λέγειν means to state, and νοεῖν to think. But what does "stating" mean? What does "thinking" mean? The dictionary which records λέγειν as stating and νοεῖν as thinking, proceeds as though the meaning of stating and thinking were the most obvious things in the world. And in a certain way, that is the case.

However, the usual case is not the case of Parmenides' saying. Nor is it the case of a translation such as a thoughtful dialogue with the saying must face.

We simply do not notice what violence and crudity we commit with the usual translation, precisely because it is correct according to the dictionary, how we turn everything upside down and throw it into confusion. It does not even occur to us that in the end, or here better in the beginning of Western thinking, the saying of Parmenides speaks to us for the first time of what is called thinking. We miss the point, therefore, if we use the word thinking in the translation. For in that way we assume that the Greek text is already speaking of thinking as if it were a fully settled matter, whereas in fact the text only leads up to the nature of thinking. We may not give "thinking" as the translation of either λέγειν taken by itself, or νοεῖν taken by itself.

Yet we have been told often enough that logic, the theory of the λόγος and its λέγειν, is the theory of thinking. Thus λέγειν taken by itself already implies "thinking." Certainly. The same holds true in the same way even of νοεῖν. For this word, too, is used by Plato and Aristotle to identify thinking.

Thinking is specifically δια-λέγεσθαι and δια-νοεῖσθαι. Both λέγειν and νοεῖν are seen as the definitive characteristics of the nature of thinking. But where and when? Only at the time, surely, when Greek thinking reaches its completion with Plato and Aristotle. But we are inquiring back into the past, are asking for that call which was first to summon λέγειν and νοεῖν to that nature which, subsequently, restricts itself to a mode whose determination will be ruled by logic as the essence of thinking.

". . . τὸ λέγειν τε νοεῖν τε: the λέγειν so (the) νοεῖν too," that is both, in their community, constitute that from which the nature of thinking first begins to emerge in one of its basic characteristics.

That the current translation has about it something unwholesome, even impossible, ought to become clear even at a superficial glance. But to make this observation, we need to make an assumption: that Parmenides was a thinker who, particularly in such a saying, would set his words down with thought and deliberation. To see the difficulty we have in mind, we must for the moment keep to the usual translation.

"Needful: the saying and so thinking, too, that being is."

This, that being is, is what is to be stated and thought. The momentous and astonishing character of the sentence "being is" has been stressed. In general, can we ever first say such a sentence and only afterward think it? Must we not on the contrary have thought the sentence first, however vaguely, so that we may then say it—assuming the word λέγειν means something vastly different from thoughtless chatter? Clearly, the saying does not require us first merely to say that being is, and then give thought to the matter afterward.

But how can the saying nonetheless mention the λέγειν *before* the νοεῖν, when both are not merely required by an indefinite "it is needful," but rather constitute what admits the "it is useful" into its essence and there holds it? We can overcome this obstacle raised by the current translation only if we translate neither λέγειν nor νοεῖν thoughtlessly, neither λέγειν with "saying" nor νοεῖν with "thinking."

However, λέγειν undeniably means to state, to report, to tell. Of course. But we come back with the question: what in the world does "stating" mean? We may not challenge that λέγειν signifies "stating." But it is just as certain that λέγειν, understood as "stating," does not mean speaking in the sense of activating the organs of speech, such as the mouth and tongue, the teeth, the larynx and the lungs and so forth.

Let us at last speak out and say what "stating" means! Let us at last give thought to *why* and in what way the Greeks designate "stating" with the word λέγειν. For λέγειν does in no way mean "to speak." The meaning of λέγειν does not necessarily refer to language and what happens in language. The verb λέγειν is the same word as the Latin *legere* and our own word *lay*. When someone lays before us a request, we do not mean that he produces papers on the desk before us, but that he speaks of the request. When someone tells of an event, he lays it out for us. When we exert ourselves, we lay to. To lay before, lay out, lay to— all this laying is the Greek λέγειν. To the Greeks, this word

does not at any time mean something like "stating," as
though the meaning came out of a blank, a void, but the
other way around: the Greeks understand stating in the
light of laying out, laying before, laying to, and *for this
reason* call that "laying" λέγειν.

The meaning of the word λόγος is determined accordingly. Parmenides himself, with all the clarity one could
wish for, tells us elsewhere what λόγος means. In fragment
7, the thinker is kept out of a dead-end way of thinking,
and is at the same time warned against the other way which
is also open, the one that mortals usually follow. But that
way of itself never leads to what is to-be-thought. However,
the warning against the usual way of mortal men does not
mean that this way is rejected. Warning is a form of preserving us from something. There speaks in the warning a
call to be careful, to have a care for something. In the text
that follows, the thinker is being warned against the usual
way of mortal men: against mistaking the common view,
which has a judgment ready beforehand on all and everything, for *the* way of thinking, just as though generalities,
and the habit of generalities, were bound to be true. The
warning runs:

"μηδέ σ᾽ ἔθος πολύπειρον ὁδὸν κατὰ τήνδε βιάσθω,
    νωμᾶν ἄσκοπον ὄμμα καὶ ἠχήεσσαν ἀκουήν
    καὶ γλῶσσαν, κρῖναι δὲ λόγωι . . ."

"And let not much-current habit force you into this way,
    to let roam sightless eyes and noise-cluttered ear
    and tongue, rather discriminate in reflection . . ."

Here λόγος is sharply contrasted with unreflecting gawking
and ear-cocking and chatter. In the text γλῶσσα, the tongue,
mere chatter, is placed in immediate and almost brutal contrast to λόγος, reflection. What is demanded here is not the
nimble tongue chattering away of all and everything, but
a λέγειν of the λόγος, and only through these the κρίνειν: to

discriminate one thing from another, to bring out one thing and put another into the background. This is the crisis that constitutes criticism.

But again we ask: what does λέγειν mean? We are far from playing etymological games when we point out: λέγειν does of course mean to state, but stating is to the Greeks in essence a laying. How curious, that stating is to be a laying? Do we intend with this reference to shake the foundations of all philology and philosophy of language, and to expose them as sham? Indeed we do. But what is laying itself? With this question, the elucidation of the essence of λέγειν as laying is merely beginning. The elucidation cannot be given here in detail (see *Logos,* a contribution to *Festschrift for Hans Jantzen, 1952,* ed. by Kurt Bauch).

When we lay something down, or out, we make it lie. Then it lies before us. But something may lie before us also without our first coming on the scene to lay it down. The sea lies before us, and the mountains. To lie, in Greek is κεῖσθαι. What lies before us is the ὑποκείμενον, in Latin *subiectum.* It might be the sea, or a village, or a house, or anything else of the kind. Only a minute fraction of what lies before us in this way has been laid down by man, and even then only with the aid of what was lying there before. The stones from which the house is built come from the natural rock.

The Greeks, however, do not think of what is lying in this sense as being in contrast with what is standing. Not just the tree that has been laid low, but also the tree that stands straight before us is something lying before us, just like the sea. The Greek word θέσις, accordingly, does not mean primarily the act of setting up, instating, but that which is set up; that which has set itself up, has settled, and as such lies before us. Θέσις is the situation in which a thing is lying.

For example, when Plato speaks of ὑποθέσεις, at the end
of the sixth book of *The Republic* where he describes the
methods of mathematics, θέσις means neither hypothesis
(assumption) in the modern sense, nor does it mean a
"mere presupposition"; rather, the ὑπόθεσις is the under-
lying foundation; the situation of the foundation, that
which is already given to and lies before the mathematicians :
the odd, the even, the shapes, the angles. These things that
lie already before us, our models, the ὑποθέσεις, are described as ὡς φανερά (510 d) : as what is evident to everybody—the things we let be.

These things that lie already before us are not, however,
what lies farther back in the sense of being remote. They
are supremely close *by*, to everything. They are what has
come close by, beforehand. But normally we fail to see them
in their presence.

Plato, however, in that famous passage, sees something
which every thinker has to see afresh each time, else he is
not a thinker : that everything that lies before us is ambiguous. This ambiguity, as we shall see, declares itself for the
first time, and definitively, in the saying of Parmenides.

Even where the meaning of the Greek θέσις comes close
to what we call setting up, and instating, even there what
has been set up always means to the Greeks that which has
come to lie, and so does lie, before us. What is set up is
released into the freedom of its station, and is not the effect
of our doing and thus dependent on us. Because of the subsequent employment made of the terms thesis, antithesis,
and synthesis—especially by Kant and German Idealism—
we hear in the word thesis at once and only the spontaneous
action and movement of the idea-forming subject. Consequently we find it difficult to hear in all its purity what the
Greek word says when θέσις still refers to lying and what
lies before us.

What is essential to lying is not that it is opposed to

standing; both in what is lying and in what is standing, the essential is that it appears, having come forward of itself. Thus we speak even today of books that have "just appeared." The book has appeared, that is, it lies before us, it is there, and in its presence it can now concern us.

Laying, λέγειν, concerns what lies there. To lay is to let lie before us. When we say something about something, we make it lie there before us, which means at the same time we make it appear. This making-to-appear and letting-lie-before-us is, in Greek thought, the essence of λέγειν and λόγος.

The essential nature of stating is not determined by the phonetic character of words as signs. The essential nature of language is illumined by the relatedness of what lies there before us to this letting-lie-before-us. However, this nature of language remains hidden from the Greeks. They have never expressly stressed it, much less raised it to the level of a problem. But their statements operate in this realm.

The relations of which we have spoken here are so weighty and far-reaching that they remain simple. This is why men overlook them constantly, with an almost unimaginable obstinacy. Our modern pundits still totally lack the sensibility to evaluate the relations we have here mentioned. To translate the λέγειν in Parmenides' saying with "the statement" is correct, according to the dictionary, but it says nothing. On the contrary, that translation embroils us in an impossible demand we must make on Parmenides: to wit, that saying is necessary first, and that thinking then has to follow after. But if we translate τὸ λέγειν in the sense we explained, then "χρὴ : τὸ λέγειν . . ." means "It is useful: to lay, let lie before us . . ."

Only now can we see our way to what follows. But even now, and more so than before, we must not translate the νοεῖν that follows with "thinking," a word which the current translation babbles as thoughtlessly as it does "saying" for λέγειν.

We shall proceed more cautiously, translating νοεῖν with "perceive," rather than say "thinking" straight out with the implication that what was said is obvious. Yet nothing is gained if in the translation of νοεῖν we now replace "thinking" with "perceive," as long as we do not become involved in what νοεῖν indicates. Above all, we must not accept "perceive" immediately as the one perfectly fitting translation, especially not if we intend "perceive" only in the sense that is reflected in the statement: "I perceive a noise."

"Perceive" here means the same thing as receive. Νοεῖν so translated—to use a Kantian distinction for the sake of convenience—is pointing toward perception in the sense of receptivity, as distinguished from the spontaneity with which we assume this or that attitude toward what we perceive. In receptive perception we remain passive, without the active attitude to what is perceived. But such passive acceptance is precisely what νοεῖν does *not* mean. This is why, in lectures I gave years ago, I insisted that νοεῖν, as perceiving, included also the active trait of undertaking something.

In νοεῖν, what is perceived concerns us in such a way that we take it up specifically, and do something with it. But where do we take what is to be perceived? How do we take it up? We take it to heart. What is taken to heart, however, is left to be exactly as it is. This taking-to-heart does not make over what is takes. Taking to heart is: to keep at heart.

Νοεῖν is taking something to heart. The noun to the verb νοεῖν, which is νόος, νοῦς, originally means almost exactly what we have explained earlier as the basic meaning of *thanc*, devotion, memory. The frequent Greek idioms ἐν νῷ ἔχειν and χαῖρε νόῳ cannot be translated with "to keep in one's reason," and "he is glad in his reason," but: χαῖρε νόῳ, he is glad at heart; ἐν νῷ ἔχειν, to keep in memory.

Summary and Transition

Χρὴ τὸ λέγειν—"It is useful, the telling . . ." What does λέγειν mean? As early as Homer, the word signifies telling a tale, and reporting. But besides, since early times and over a wide area, in all its many variants and derivations it means as much as laying. It can easily be confirmed that λέγειν means both telling and laying. The two meanings are so far apart that they do not interfere with each other. Λόγος, a word that later attains the supreme heights of theological speculation, and λέχος, a word that designates so common an object as a couch, have after all nothing to do with each other. Why, then, should we be troubled by the undeniable multiplicity of meanings of the word λέγειν? We are so busy anyhow with routine that we imagine the course of the world, too, can be controlled with routine measures.

On the other hand, we may become thoughtful in face of the fact that λέγειν means both stating and laying. To modern man, such thoughtfulness will of course seem entirely out of place, not to say eccentric—and in any event useless. Yet modern man will perhaps forgive us for reminding him that this remarkable word λέγειν, λόγος—or rather what it signifies—is at the root of Western logic.

Without the λέγειν of that logic, modern man would have to make do without his automobile. There would be no airplanes, no turbines, no Atomic Energy Commission. Without the λέγειν and its λόγος, Christianity would not have the doctrine of the Trinity, nor the theological interpretation of the concept of the second Person of the Trinity. Without the λέγειν and its λόγος, there would have been no Age of Enlightenment. Without this λέγειν, there would be no dialectical materialism. Without the λόγος, of logic, the world would look different. But it is idle to speculate on how the world would then look.

But is it not just as idle to go into this undeniable peculiarity of the Greek word λέγειν, that it means at one time "to lay," and at another time "to tell"? It is idle. It is even useless—and what is useless belongs no place. Thus it is out of place wherever it appears. This fact has peculiar consequences. We do not here make the claim that we are capable of dealing with the useless; we only raise the possibility that a discussion of λέγειν as "laying" and "telling" might at some time be of some little use. And so, in the end, we ask once again.

We ask: what is it that takes place when λέγειν means both "to lay" and "to tell"? Is it only by accident that these meanings come together under the common roof of the same word-sound? Or is there something else? Could it be that that which is the essence of telling, that which is called λέγειν, has come to light as a laying? In what essential form does language come to light, when its statement is taken over and accomplished as a laying?

We must thus first of all make clear what laying means. It is remarkable that we must first clarify something like laying, something we do daily and hourly in many ways. The thing that matters when we lay something, the thing by which laying comes to be laying, is this: what must be laid lies there, and henceforth belongs to what *already* lies before us. And what lies before us is primary, especially when it lies there *before* all the laying and setting that are *man's* work, when it lies there prior to all that man lays out, lays down, or lays in ruin.

To the Greeks, telling is laying. Language has its essential being in the telling. If to the Greeks the nature of the poetic tale is determined by the laying, it must be that laying and lying and what lies before them lies close to their heart, so definitively that to the Greek even that which *is*, and not only the statement of it, reveals itself and is determined by the laying and the lying. Sea and mountains, city and island, temple and sky lie before man and emerge into appearance as they lie there.

When man finds himself among what so lies before him, should he not respond to it in all purity by letting it lie before him just as it lies? And this letting-lie, would it not be that laying which is the stage for all the other laying that man performs? Thus laying would now suddenly emerge as a relatedness that pervades man's stay on this earth from the ground up—though we have never asked where this relatedness originates. Then λέγειν, as a laying and a letting-lie, would be something uncanny in the midst of all the current canniness of human existence?

And λέγειν as a telling? Telling is the business of language. What does language tell? What language tells, what it speaks and what it keeps silent, is and remains always and everywhere what is, what can be, what has been, and what is about to come—most directly and abundantly where the terms "is" and "be" are not specifically given voice. For whatever is put into language in any real sense is essentially richer than what is captured in audible and visible phonetic conformations, and as such falls silent again when it is put in writing. But even so, every statement remains in a mysterious manner related to all that can be called up by a "There is . . ."

"There is a light that the wind has put out.
    There is an inn on the heath which a drunkard leaves in the afternoon.
    There is a vineyard, burnt and black with holes full of spiders.
    There is a room which they have white-washed with milk.
    The madman has died . . ."

This is not written in a textbook of logic, but elsewhere. Laying, thought as a letting-lie in the widest sense, re-

lates to what in the widest sense lies before us, and speaks
without a sound : there is.

To lay and to tell relate in the same mode to the same, in
the mode of a letting-appear. Telling turns out to be a laying, and is called λέγειν.

Χρὴ τὸ λέγειν τε . . . "Useful is the letting-lie-before-
us also νοεῖν." This word νοεῖν does not originally mean
"thinking" any more than does λέγειν. The two have become joined in closest kinship only by virtue of their original nature, and are later reduced to what logic transacts as
the essence of thinking. Νοεῖν implies a perceiving which
never was nor is a mere receiving of something. The νοεῖν
perceives beforehand by taking to mind and heart. The
heart is the wardship guarding what lies before us, though
this wardship itself needs that guarding which is accomplished in the λέγειν as gathering. Νόος and νοῦς, therefore,
do not originally signify what later develops into reason;
νόος signifies the minding that has something in mind and
takes it to heart. Thus νοεῖν also means what we understand
by scenting—though we use the word mostly of animals,
in nature.

Man's scenting is divination. But since by now we understand all knowledge and all skill in terms of the thinking
of logic, we measure "divination" by the same yardstick.
But the word means more. Authentic divination is the
mode in which essentials come to us and so come to mind,
in order that we may keep them in mind. This kind of
divination is not the outer court before the gates of knowledge. It is the great hall where everything that can be
known is kept, concealed.

We translate νοεῖν with "take to heart."

"χρὴ τὸ λέγειν τε νοεῖν τε . . ."
"Useful is the letting-lie-before-us also (the) taking-to-
    heart too . . ."

LECTURE
IX

———◆◆———

We translate λέγειν with letting-lie-before-us, and νοεῖν with taking-to-heart. This translation is not only more appropriate but also clearer. We shall set the essentials down, and apart, in four points.

(1) The translation clarifies why and in what way λέγειν precedes νοεῖν and therefore is mentioned first. Letting things lie before us is necessary to supply us with what, lying thus before us, can be taken to heart. Λέγειν is prior to νοεῖν, and not only because it has to be accomplished first in order that νοεῖν may find something it can take to heart. Rather, λέγειν also surpasses νοεῖν, in that it once again gathers, and keeps and safeguards in the gathering, whatever νοεῖν takes to heart; for λέγειν, being a laying, is also *legere*, that is, reading. We normally understand by reading only this, that we grasp and follow a script and written matter. But that is done by gathering the letters. Without this gathering, without a gleaning in the sense in which wheat or grapes are gleaned, we should never be able to read a single word, however keenly we observe the written signs. (2) Thus λέγειν and νοεῖν are coordinated not only in series, first λέγειν then νοεῖν, but each enters into the other. Λέγειν, the letting-lie-before-us, unfolds of its own accord into the νοεῖν. What we are talking about here is anything but leaving something where it lies while we pass

by indifferently. For instance, when we let the sea lie before us as it lies, we, in λέγειν, are already engaged in keeping in mind and heart what lies before us. We have already taken to heart what lies before us. Λέγειν is tacitly disposed to νοεῖν.

Conversely, νοεῖν always remains a λέγειν. When we take to heart what lies before us, we take it as it is lying. By taking to heart and mind, we gather and focus ourselves on what lies before us, and gather what we have taken to heart. Whence do we gather it? Where else but to itself, so that it may become manifest such as it of itself lies before us. The language of the saying is indeed exceedingly careful. It does not just tie λέγειν to νοεῖν by a mere καί, "and"; rather, the saying runs: τὸ λέγειν τε νοεῖν τε. This τε——τε has a reflexive meaning, and says: the letting-lie-before-us and the taking-to-heart enter upon and into one another, in a give-and-take. The relation between λέγειν and νοεῖν is not a patchwork of things and attitudes otherwise alien to each other. The relation is a conjunction, and what is joined here is, each of itself, related to, that is, connatural with the other. Accordingly, we translate τὸ λέγειν τε νοεῖν τε: the letting-lie-before-us such (as this), the taking-to-heart too (such as the other). (3) This translation does not just bring out more appropriately the meaning of the two words λέγειν and νοεῖν; it alone makes the entire saying audible in what it says. The saying does not presuppose what is called thinking, but first indicates the fundamental traits of what subsequently defines itself as thinking. The conjunction of λέγειν and νοεῖν first announces what is called thinking. The possible restriction of thinking, to the concept of thinking established by logic, is here only in preparation. Λέγειν and νοεῖν, both by virtue of their conjunction, achieve what later, and only for a short time, is specifically called ἀληθεύειν: to disclose and keep disclosed what is unconcealed.

The veiled nature of λέγειν and νοεῖν lies in this, that

they correspond to the unconcealed and its unconcealedness. Here we receive an intimation of how χρή, which governs the conjunction of λέγειν and νοεῖν, is expressed through ᾽Αλήθεια. To make us see this more clearly would require a translation of the entire opening section of what is usually called Parmenides' *Didactic Poem*. But first we must give thought to something else; something that leads up to what has been intimated, and what, without being specifically discussed, illumines the matter indicated at the end of our lectures.

The conjunction of λέγειν and νοεῖν, however, is such that it does not rest upon itself. Letting-lie-before-us and taking-to-heart in themselves point toward something that touches and only thereby fully defines them. Therefore, the essential nature of thinking cannot be adequately defined either by λέγειν, taken alone, or by νοεῖν, taken alone, or again by both together taken as a conjunction.

Later on, that course is taken nonetheless. Thinking becomes the λέγειν of the λόγος in the sense of proposition. At the same time, thinking becomes the νοεῖν in the sense of apprehension by reason. The two definitions are coupled together, and so determine what is henceforth called thinking in the Western-European tradition.

The coupling of λέγειν and νοεῖν, as proposition and as reason, are distilled into what the Romans call *ratio*. Thinking appears as what is rational. *Ratio* comes from the verb *reor*. *Reor* means to take something for something—νοεῖν; and this is at the same time to state something as something —λέγειν. *Ratio* becomes reason. Reason is the subject matter of logic. Kant's main work, the *Critique of Pure Reason*, deals with the critique of pure reason by way of logic and dialectic.

But the original nature of λέγειν and νοεῖν, disappears in *ratio*. As *ratio* assumes dominion, all relations are turned around. For medieval and modern philosophy now explain the *Greek* essence of λέγειν and νοεῖν, λόγος and νοῦς in terms of their own concept of *ratio*. That explanation, however, no longer enlightens—it obfuscates. The Enlightenment obscures the essential origin of thinking. In general, it blocks every access to the thinking of the Greeks. But that is not to say that philosophy after the Greeks is false and a mistake. It is to say at most that philosophy, despite all logic and all dialectic, does not attain to the discussion of the question "What is called thinking?" And philosophy strays farthest from this hidden question when it is led to think that thinking must begin with doubting. (4) If we now listen still more carefully than before, for what λέγειν and νοεῖν state in the translation; if we search the conjunction of the two for a first glimmer of the essential traits of thinking—then we shall be extremely careful not to take what the saying states forthwith for a rigid definition of thinking. If we continue to be careful, we shall instead find something curious. It will strike us as strange—and that impression must in no way be softened.

Νοεῖν, taking-to-heart, is determined by λέγειν. This means two things:

First, νοεῖν unfolds out of λέγειν. Taking is not grasping, but letting come what lies before us.

Second, νοεῖν is kept within λέγειν. The heart into which it takes things belongs to the gathering where what lies before us is safeguarded and kept as such.

The conjunction of λέγειν and νοεῖν is the fundamental characteristic of thinking which here moves into its essential nature. Thinking, then, is not a grasping, neither the grasp of what lies before us, nor an attack upon it. In λέγειν and νοεῖν, what lies before us is not manipulated by means of grasping. Thinking is not grasping or prehending. In the high youth of its unfolding essence, thinking knows nothing of the grasping concept (*Begriff*). The reason is not at all that thinking was then undeveloped. Rather, evolving thinking is not yet confined within limits that limit it by setting bounds to the evolving of its essential nature. The confinement which follows later is then, of course, not considered a loss or a defect, but rather the sole gain that thinking has to offer once its work is accomplished by means of the concept.

But all of the great thinking of the Greek thinkers, including Aristotle, thinks non-conceptually. Does it therefore think inaccurately, hazily? No, the very opposite: it thinks appropriately, as befits the matter. Which is to say also: thinking keeps to its way of thinking. It is the way toward what is worthy of questioning, problematical. What particular beings in their Being might be, still remains an everlasting question even for Aristotle. At the end of my book on *Kant and the Problem of Metaphysics* (1929), I call attention to a long-forgotten statement from Aristotle's treatises on *Metaphysics*, which runs:

"καὶ δὴ καὶ τὸ πάλαι τε καὶ νῦν καὶ ἀεὶ ζητούμενον καὶ ἀεὶ ἀπορούμενον τί τὸ ὄν . . ."

"And so it remains something to be looked for, from of old and now and forever, and thus something that offers no way out: what is being . . . ?"

It profits nothing, of course, that we now quote this statement of Aristotle again, if we neglect to hear that it relentlessly insists on our taking the road into what is problematical. His persistence in that questioning attitude separates the thinker Aristotle by an abyss from all that Aristotelianism which, in the manner of all followers, falsifies what is problematical and so produces a clear-cut counterfeit answer. And where no counterfeit answer is produced, what is problematical becomes merely questionable. The questionable then appears as something uncertain, weak, and fragile, something that is threatening to fall apart. We now need some assurance that will put everything together again in comprehensible security. This reassuring combination is the system, σύστημα. The systematic and system-building way of forming ideas through concepts takes control.

Concept and system alike are alien to Greek thinking. Greek thinking, therefore, remains of a fundamentally different kind from the more modern ways of thinking of Kierkegaard and Nietzsche who, to be sure, think in opposition to the system, but for that very reason remain the system's captives. By way of Hegelian metaphysics, Kierkegaard remains everywhere philosophically entangled, on the one hand in a dogmatic Aristotelianism that is completely on a par with medieval scholasticism, and on the other in the subjectivity of German idealism. No discerning mind would deny the stimuli produced by Kierkegaard's thought that prompted us to give renewed attention to the "existential." But about the decisive question—the essential nature of Being—Kierkegaard has nothing whatever to say.

But we must here give attention to another matter. The interpretation of Greek thinking that is guided by modern conceptual thinking not only remains inappropriate for Greek thinking; it also keeps us from hearing the appeal of the problematic of Greek thinking, and thus from being held to a constantly more urgent summons to go on questioning. We must not fail, of course, to reflect on why and in what way it was precisely the thinking of the Greeks that essentially prepared the development of thinking in the sense of forming conceptual ideas; indeed, Greek thinking was bound to suggest that development. But on the path which we are following here, the important thing for us is first to see that our modern way of representational ideas, as long as it stubbornly holds to its way, blocks its own access to the beginning and thus to the fundamental characteristic of Western thinking. The translations alone make this point clear:

We now translate

"χρὴ : τὸ λέγειν τε νοεῖν τε . . ."

with

"Useful is: the letting-lie-before-us so (the) taking-to-heart too . . ."

But λέγειν and νοεῖν is useful not just in general and by and large, as though we were dealing merely with an invitation to be attentive whenever we form ideas, as though the saying, expressed in terms of the usual translation, intended to say: it is necessary that we think. On the contrary, the saying is leading toward the first flash of dawn of the nature of thinking.

But what, in turn, determines that nature? What else but that to which λέγειν and νοεῖν refer? And that is identified in the word immediately following. The word is ἐόν. Ἐόν is translated as "being." Later, the word is merely ὄν. The epsilon disappears, but this vowel epsilon is precisely what gives the root of the word: ἐ, ἐς, ἔστιν, est, "is." We do not translate ἐόν with "the being" because there is no article. The lack of the article further increases the strangeness. Ἐόν specifies That by which the letting-lie-before-us and the taking-to-heart are engaged.

Ἐόν, being—the translation is once again just as correct according to the dictionary as the translation of λέγειν with "telling." And we understand the translation, "being," without the least difficulty—at least as long as our ideas and our views remain unquestioning, average, common.

Summary and Transition

The title of this lecture course is a question. The question runs: What is called thinking? As a course of lectures, we expect it to answer the question. As the course proceeds, then, it would make the title disappear bit by bit. But the title of our lecture course remains—because it is intended as it sounds. It remains the title of the entire course. That course remains one single question: What is it that calls on us to think? What is That which calls us into thinking?

By the way we have chosen, we are trying to trace the call by which Western-European thinking is summoned and directed to that which is consummated as thinking.

We are trying to hear the call for which we ask, in a saying of Parmenides that says:

"χρὴ τὸ λέγειν τε νοεῖν τε"
"Useful is the λέγειν so also the νοεῖν."

Later on, with Plato and Aristotle, the two terms signify —each by itself—what subsequent philosophy understands by thinking.

But if we, following the later tradition, translate λέγειν and νοεῖν in Parmenides' saying straight away into "thinking," we then get in the way of our own purpose. For we are after all trying first to detect in that saying to what fundamental traits of its own essential nature thinking is called. This is why we translate λέγειν literally with: letting-lie-before-us, and νοεῖν, on the other hand, with: taking-to-heart. Both belong to one single mutual conjunction. But even this conjunction does not yet distinguish the fundamental character of thinking.

The conjunction in its turn requires the determination by that to which it complies. What is that? Quite clearly That to which λέγειν and νοεῖν refer. The saying names it in the word that immediately follows. That word is: ἐόν. The translation, correct by the dictionary, is: being. Everybody understands the word, at least by and large and for everyday use, if indeed the word is ever spoken in everyday language.

LECTURE
X

———————◆———————

If we were to examine what everyman has in mind each time he hears or repeats the word "being," we would gather most varied and most curious information. We would have to face up to a strange confusion, and probably to recognize that the notorious chaos of the state of the world today expresses itself even in such inconspicuous fields as the range of meanings this word seems to have. In fact, that chaos may even have its roots here. But a still greater puzzle is that men nonetheless understand each other. All things are reduced to a common denominator, which then nominates for us what is so commonly understood by a "being." We are always able to point out directly, by all kinds of simple indications, what the word "being" means. We point to the mountains, the sea, the forest, the horse, the ship, the sky, God, the contest, the people's assembly. And those indications are correct.

But then, how is anyone to understand what is the use of a Greek saying that says: "*Useful* is the letting-lie-before-us . . ." of what lies before us. Λέγειν, the letting-lie-before-us, becomes just as superfluous as the νοεῖν which follows. For mortal men perceive automatically and constantly what lies before them. As they move on the land they observe the mountains, and as they sail, the sea. They observe the signs in the sky, and are attentive to the signs given by God. They observe each other in the contest. They watch each other at the feast and in the popular assembly. The letting-lie-before-us, and the observing of the ἐόν, happen by themselves, simply because such living beings as men exist. Men do not first need a special summons to λέγειν and νοεῖν. Nor do they know anything about it.

And yet the saying speaks out and says: "χρή—Useful is the letting-lie-before-us so (the) taking-to-heart too: ἐόν, being." However, the saying does not end with ἐόν. The last word in the saying is given to the last word that the saying says: ἐόν ἔμμεναι. The infinitive ἔμμεναι is, like ἔσμεναι, an older form for εἶναι, and means: to be.

"Useful is: letting-lie-before-us and so (the) taking-to-heart too: being: to be."

What are we talking about when we now use these terms? We are dealing with them as if they were empty shells. "Being" and "to be" are almost no more than empty sounds. We have, besides, some historical knowledge that philosophy from of old uses these words to identify the theme with which it struggles. We are in a peculiar position.

On the one hand, the words "being" and "to be" say nothing graspable. On the other hand, they are the highest rubrics of philosophy. But these same rubrics, when used with emphasis, strike us as alien substances in the language. They disturb the harmonious and artless progress of natural speech. Ultimately, there is a chill around these terms. We do not quite know where the chill comes from—whether it comes from what they indicate, or from the frozen, spectral manner in which they haunt all philosophical discourse and writing. All this will cause misery to a man who is honest with himself, who will not let himself be confused by all the uproar about Being and Existence.

With such miserable means as the vaporous and empty terms "being" and "to be," how can we meet the demands of the translation of Parmenides' saying, specifically the translation of his final words on which everything clearly depends?

The final words are ἐόν : ἔμμεναι. The saying is to tell us what it is that calls mortals to thinking, by involving and directing them into the fundamental elements of thinking, into the conjunction of λέγειν and νοεῖν. But for the moment we hear only this much in the saying, that λέγειν and νοεῖν in their turn refer to ἐόν : ἔμμεναι. Ἐόν : ἔμμεναι is, so to speak, the object of their reference. Is it mere accident that λέγειν and νοεῖν have come upon this object which is no object? Probably not. For the first word of the saying says χρή : "It is useful . . ."

But why, and in what way, do letting-lie-before-us and taking-to-heart refer to ἐὸν ἔμμεναι, to "being," to "to be"? The reference is useful. To whom or what is this reference useful, of λέγειν and νοεῖν to ἐὸν ἔμμεναι? Does "being," does "to be" have use for the letting-lie-before-us and the taking-to-heart?

Being can be, can it not, without there being men who take it to heart? For a long time now, talk has gone around that being is "in itself." Is such talk, too, "in itself"? Or is it, together with its thought content, subject to a call? Does the call which calls us into thinking issue from being, or from Being, or from both, or from neither? Is the ἐὸν ἔμμεναι, contrary to appearances, *more* than just the object for λέγειν and νοεῖν? Is ἐὸν ἔμμεναι, is "being," is "to be" perhaps much rather the subject which draws all λέγειν and νοεῖν to itself, refers it to itself—and does so of necessity? However, when we are talking here of "object" and "subject," we are using only the crudest makeshift to indicate the relation which is now emerging in the distance.

To gain clarity, to be able merely to ask the proper ques-

tions in the matter, we must surely first make clear what
the Greek words ἐόν and ἔμμεναι signify. What they indicate presumably belongs together. Even linguistically, "being" and "to be" are no more than different forms of the
same word. They designate, so it seems, the same thing.

We can stress and specify that the two words belong together, and still not be able to think properly what is designated by the words. Indeed, we must give particular attention to the manner in which they belong together, if we are
to hear Parmenides' saying at all in the proper way.

Fortunately, Parmenides himself, by his manner of stating, gives us a hint which helps us to bring out the manner
in which ἐόν and ἔμμεναι, "being" and "to be," belong
together.

For Parmenides elsewhere frequently uses the word ἐόν
for ἔμμεναι, εἶναι. At first glance, and especially in the light
of the saying we are discussing, that seems strange. But in
substance, that usage has good grounds, as good as anything
can have. If we substitute the usage just mentioned, ἐόν, for
ἔμμεναι, the saying runs:

"χρὴ τὸ λέγειν τε νοεῖν τ᾿ ἐὸν ἐόν."

According to the wording, the same thing is now said twice
—and thus nothing at all is said. That is, unless the same
word ἐόν says different things in the first and the second
place. And so it does. This is possible only if one and the
same word, ἐόν, has two different meanings. But does not
every word have more than one meaning? Doubtless. The
multiple meanings of the word ἐόν, however, are neither
accidental nor vague. Rather, the word has two meanings
in a specific and distinctive sense.

A grammatical reflection is needed to make the point
clear. What reservations there are concerning the extent of
its validity will become obvious in what follows.

The word "being," by its structure, sounds and speaks

like the terms "blossoming," "gleaming," "resting," "aching," and so on. The grammatical name of long standing for words so formed is *participle*. They participate, they take part—in two meanings. But the essential point is not that there are only two meanings, instead of three or four, but that the two meanings refer to each other. Each of the two meanings is one of the pair. The word "blossoming" can mean: the given something that is blossoming—the rosebush or apple tree. If the word is intended in this sense, it designates what stands in bloom. "Blossoming" designates the given something that is blossoming, and intends this something by itself as that to which blossoming is fitting and proper. The word "blossoming," if it means, for instance, the rose, here almost represents the proper name for what it designates. In its linguistic form, it has the character of a substantive, a noun. "Blossoming," so understood, is used as a noun.

But blossoming may also mean "the act of blossoming," in contrast with "the act of wilting." What is meant is not the given plant that happens to be blossoming or wilting, but "blossoming, wilting." Here "blossoming" is used in its verbal sense.

Participles take part in both the nominal and the verbal meaning. This is something we learn in grammar school. We do not give it much thought. But at this time, and in this place, it is no longer sufficient to point out that participles have two meanings—as though all we had to do were to classify the word in question, ἐόν, being, as a participle. That classification is correct, of course, if we are content with grammar and with the fact that such words happen to exist in this linguistic form. Blossoming, that is something blossoming and the act of blossoming; flowing, that is something flowing and the act of flowing, and accordingly, then, "being" means something in being, and the act of being.

But why do participles have two meanings? Is it because they take part in two meanings? No, rather these words are participles because what they state is always applied to what is in itself twofold. Blossoming in its meaning as a noun designates a being that is blossoming. Blossoming in its meaning as a verb designates "to be in bloom." When the word is used in its nominal meaning, "something blossoming," it is no longer specifically stated that this something is, of course, a being; and no more does the word "to be" find expression when the word "blossoming" is used as a verb. What is the upshot of all this?

The participle ἐόν, being, is not just *one more* participle among countless others; ἐόν, *ens*, being is the participle which gathers all other possible participles into itself. The dual meaning of participles stems from the duality of what they tacitly designate. But this dualism in its turn stems from a *distinctive* duality that is concealed in the word ἐόν, being. One might suppose that participles like blossoming, sounding, flowing, aching are concrete, while the participle ἐόν, being, is always abstract. The opposite is true.

The participle in which all the rest have their roots, in which they grow together (*concrescere*), and from which they continuously grow, though without specifically expressing it, is that participle which speaks from a unique and therefore distinctive duality. In keeping with that dual nature, a being has its being in Being, and Being persists as the Being of a being. There does not exist another kind of twofoldness that can compare with this.

"Participle" is a grammatical term. What it refers to, fundamentally though not explicitly, is that duality which, linguistically and grammatically, by way of the words ἐόν, ὄν, *ens*, being, is counted as apparently one among all the other participles. The grammarians of ancient Rome took their terms for the various word forms from the Greek grammarians. The investigations of the Greek grammarians were based on those designations of language that resulted from the reflections of logic on λόγος and λεκτόν. And those reflections of logic, in their turn, go back to the philosophy of Plato and Aristotle.

Thus, our current distinction between nouns and action words, substantives and verbs, does not arise from grammar. Nor does it come out of logic textbooks. It comes to light for the first time, deliberately and laboriously, in one of the most profound dialogues Plato has left us, the "Sophist." The Latin term *participium* is the translation of the Greek μετοχή. The taking part of something in something is called μετέχειν. This word is fundamental to Plato's thinking. It designates the participation of any given being in that through which it—say, this table—shows its face and form (in Greek, ἰδέα or εἶδος) as this being. In this appearance it is in present being, it *is*. According to Plato, the idea constitutes the Being of a being. The idea is the face whereby a given something shows its form, looks at us, and thus appears, for instance, as this table. In this form, the thing looks at us.

Now Plato designates the relation of a given being to its idea as μέθεξις, participation. But this participation of the one, the being, in the other, the Being, already *presupposes* that the duality of being and Being does exist. Μέθεξις, the participation of beings in Being, consists in what the μετοχή, the participle ἐόν, ὄν, designates grammatically.

In Aristotle's statement cited earlier, we learned that the persistent question of thinking is: τί τὸ ὄν—what is the particular being in its Being? The struggle to answer this unique question determines the fundamental character of the history of philosophy.

Western-European thinking, in keeping with the guiding question τί τὸ ὄν, what is the particular being in its Being?, proceeds from beings to Being. Thinking ascends from the former to the latter. In keeping with the guiding question, thinking transcends the particular being, in the direction of its Being, not in order to leave behind and abandon the particular being, but so that by this ascent, this transcendence, it may represent the particular being in that which it, *as* a being, is.

What of itself lies before us, the particular being, is to the Greeks that which arises of itself (Φύσις), and thus can be called the "physical." This word is taken broadly here, to include the psychic and the spiritual as well. The guiding question—what is being, what is the physical in the widest sense?—goes beyond the particular being. "Going beyond one thing to another" is in Greek μετά. Thinking in the sense of the question τί τὸ ὄν—what is the particular being in respect of its Being?—thus takes a peculiar turn under the name "metaphysics." The thematic sphere of Western metaphysics is indicated by μέθεξις, the particular being's participation in Being; so that the question is now how the participating being can be defined in terms of Being. This sphere of metaphysics is grounded in what μετοχή, what the unique participle ἐόν designates with a single word: the duality of individual beings and Being. But in order that metaphysical thinking may first of all discern its own sphere, and attempt its first steps in that sphere,

"χρὴ τὸ λέγειν τε νοεῖν τ᾽ἐὸν ἐόν"
"It is useful to let-lie-before-us and so the taking-to-heart also: beings in being."

The duality of individual beings and Being must first lie before us openly, be taken to heart and there kept safely, before it can be conceived and dealt with in the sense of the participation of the one, a particular being, in the other, Being.

What is the call that speaks to us from Parmenides' saying? "Let lie before you, and take to heart, ἐὸν ἔμμεναι, beings in being!"

In terms of grammar later on, and thus seen from the outside, Parmenides' saying says: take to heart ἐόν as participle, and with it take heed of ἔμμεναι in ἐόν, the Being of beings. However, *no* further inquiry and thought is given to the duality *itself*, of beings and Being, neither to the nature of the duality nor to that nature's origin. The duality emerges only up to the point where the ἔμμεναι of ἐόν, the Being of beings, can be taken to heart. Thus it is that the one thing which remains to be asked—what are particular beings in their Being?—comes to the fore within the sphere of this duality. The style of all Western-European philosophy—and there is no other, neither a Chinese nor an Indian philosophy—is determined by this duality "beings—in being." Philosophy's procedure in the sphere of this duality is decisively shaped by the interpretation Plato gave to the duality. That the duality appears as participation does not at all go without saying.

In order that a Western-European metaphysics can arise, in order that a meta-physical thinking can become the mission and historic fate of mortal man, is necessary before all else that a call summon us into the λέγειν τε νοεῖν τ'ἐὸν ἔμμεναι.

Accordingly—what is called "thinking," insofar as it follows this call? Thinking means: letting-lie-before-us and so taking-to-heart also: beings in being. Thinking so structured pervades the foundation of metaphysics, the duality of beings and Being. Such thinking develops its various successive positions on this foundation, and determines the fundamental positions of metaphysics.

Does the saying, then, provide us with an answer after all to the question what is to be understood by thinking? No. If we hear it rightly, it only helps us to question. The saying, however, does tell us what will be useful to us—this humble and simple λέγειν τε νοεῖν τ'ἐὸν ἔμμεναί.

The appropriate translation of the saying must therefore

run: "Useful to let-lie-before-us so (the) taking-to-heart also: beings in being."

This translation makes clear how the relation of the infinitive ἔμμεναι to the participle ἐόν is to be understood. But does that alone give us the needed clarity about what "being," "in being," and "to be" designate? Clearly not.

Yet the terms "being" and "to be" have long since played the role of decisive rubrics in the conceptual language of philosophy. The much-vaunted *philosophia perennis*, which is to outlast the centuries, would crumble in its foundations if the language of these rubrics were taken away from it. If we stop for a moment and attempt, directly and precisely and without subterfuge, to represent in our minds what the terms "being" and "to be" state, we find that *such an examination has nothing to hold onto*. All our ideas slip away and dissolve in vagueness. Not entirely, though, because there always echoes, dark and confused, something of the kind that is vouchsafed to our opinions and propositions. If it were otherwise, we could never in any way understand what we nonetheless constantly repeat at present: "This summer is hot."

Let us imagine in thought once again and once more that this inconspicuous little "is" could not be thought. What would become of our stay in the world, if this firm and constantly affirmed "is" were denied us?

And yet, to make clear what "to be" says we need only point to some being—a mountain, a house lying before us, a tree standing there. What do we point out when we help ourselves by such indications? We indicate a being, of course; but strictly speaking the indication comes to rest on the mountain, the house, the tree. Now we imagine that we have the answer to precisely what is still in question. For we do not, after all, inquire about a being as mountain, as house, as tree, as though we wanted to climb a mountain, move into a house, or plant a tree. We inquire about the mountain, about the house, about the tree as a given being, in order to give thought to the being of the mountain, the being of the house, the being of the tree.

We notice at once, it is true, that being is not attached to the mountain somewhere, or stuck to the house, or hanging from the tree. We notice, thus, the problematic that is designated with "being." Our question therefore becomes more questioning. We let beings, as beings, lie before us and give our heart and mind to the "being" of particular beings.

But so long as that which the words ἐόν and ἔμμεναι state dissolves in the vague terms "beings" and "to be," we cannot hear what the saying says. For these terms offer no guarantee that they carry *across* to us what the Greek ἐὸν ἔμμεναι tells. The translation is still no translation if we merely replace the words ἐόν and ἔμμεναι with our own terms "being" and "to be," or the Latin *ens* and *esse*.

What, then, is still missing in the traditional translation of the words ἐόν with "being" and ἔμμεναι with "to be"? What is missing is that we did not try to say those words over in the same way as we did the words χρή and λέγειν and νοεῖν, and the particles τε . . . τε. What is still needed? That we ourselves, instead of merely transposing the Greek terms into terms of our language, pass over into the Greek sphere of ἐόν and ἔμμεναι, ὄν and εἶναι. This passage is hard—not in itself, only for us. But it is not impossible.

Summary and Transition

Parmenides' saying moves toward that which is designated by the word ἐόν. This fact becomes quite clear if, on the strength of Parmenides' own usage, we replace the final word ἔμμεναι with ἐόν. In grammatical terms, the word is a participle. Reflection showed that ἐόν is the participle of all participles. Ἐόν is the unique and thus distinctive μετοχή. It tells of the duality: beings in being; being of individual beings. Instead of the verbal signification, language also uses the infinitive ἔμμεναι, εἶναι, esse, to be.

The well-worn form of ἐόν, current in the writing of Plato and Aristotle, is ὄν, τὸ ὄν, beings in being. All of Western metaphysics, without suffering the least violence, could be placed under the title: τὸ ὄν. If we do so, we must meet one condition, however. From the outset, and constantly and exclusively, we must hear and read the word τὸ ὄν as the distinctive participle, even if we do not always make it explicit in philosophical parlance.

When we say "Being," it means "Being of beings." When we say "beings," it means "beings in respect of Being." We are always speaking *within* the duality. The duality is always a prior datum, for Parmenides as much as for Plato, Kant as much as Nietzsche. The duality has developed beforehand the sphere within which the relation of beings to Being becomes capable of being mentally represented. That relation can be interpreted and explained in various ways.

An interpretation decisive for Western thought is that given by Plato. He says that between beings and Being there prevails the χωρισμός; ἡ χώρα is the *locus*, the site, the place. Plato means to say: beings and Being are in different places. Particular beings and Being are differently located. Thus when Plato gives thought to the different location of beings and Being, he is asking for the totally different place of Being, as against the place of beings.

To make the question of the χωρισμός, the *difference* in placement of beings and Being at all possible, the *distinction*—the duality of the two—must be given beforehand, in such a way that this duality itself does not as such receive specific attention.

The same is true for all transcendence. When we pass

from beings to Being, our passage passes through the duality of the two. But the passage never first creates the duality. The duality is already in use. It is the thing most used, and thus most usual, in all our stating and ideas, in all we do.

If we hear the word έόν in its dual signification, by virtue of its grammatical, participial form, we now can translate the saying more clearly:

> "Useful is the letting-lie-before-us, so (the) taking-to-heart, too: beings in being."

But this, too, is still not a translation of the final words of the saying. We have merely replaced the Greek words with others, with *ens* and *esse* or with "being" and "to be." But this replacement business does not lead us anywhere. If we are to hear the saying, if we are to be prompted by it to raise questions, it is not enough to exchange the Greek words for other words in other languages, however familiar. Instead, what is needed is that we let the Greek words tell us directly what *they* designate. We must transplant our hearing to where the telling statement of the Greek language has its domain.

LECTURE
XI

◆

What does ἐὸν ἔμμεναι mean, thought in Greek? This is the question at which we now arrive by way of the question "What is called thinking?" How does it happen that the question about thinking leads us to give thought to what the Greeks may mean when they say ἐόν (being), and ἔμμεναι (to be)?

The question "What is called thinking?" faced us at the beginning of our way, in four modes.

What is called thinking? means most immediately and first: what does this word "thinking" signify? We learned that it signifies memory, thanks, thinking that recalls. Since then, we have heard no more of such matters along our way.

What is called thinking? means further and second: what, according to the long traditional doctrine of thinking, logic, do we still today understand by thinking? Though no particulars were given on the teachings of logic, we noted that the name logic corresponds to what this doctrine understands by thinking. Thinking is λέγειν, λόγος in the sense of proposition, that is, of judgment. Judging is thought to be the activity of the understanding in the broad sense of reason. The perception of reason traces back to νοεῖν. Parmenides' saying told us about the judgment of

229

reason, about λέγειν in connection with νοεῖν. The saying deals neither with the λόγος of logic, nor with the judgments of reason, but only with the conjunction of λέγειν and νοεῖν. The letting-lie-before-us and (the) taking-to-heart emerge so far only as the basic character of what subsequently is called thinking and is viewed in terms of logic.

Thus our attempt to translate Parmenides' saying did in a certain sense yield us an answer to the second question. Accordingly, what is called thinking is, properly, letting-lie-before-us and so taking-to-heart also. . . . But it turned out that this definition of thinking is far from adequate. Something is still lacking in the definition, and that something is no less than the main thing, that is, the indication of what λέγειν and νοεῖν refer to. Only that indication will allow us to ask adequately: What is called thinking? And that to which the conjunction of λέγειν and νοεῖν joins and conforms itself is the ἐὸν ἔμμεναι. And what ἐὸν ἔμμεναι means, thought in Greek terms, is the question at which we stop. This means that our seemingly wayward effort to make an appropriate translation of ἐὸν ἔμμεναι, the final words of the saying, has the sole purpose of bringing this question into focus: what, according to tradition, is really called thinking?

Our lecture course has tried to follow this question—but not by detaching this second way of asking from the whole of the four questions. Instead, the second way of asking was from the start subordinated to the decisive way in which the question "What is called thinking?" remains to be asked. That way is: what is That which directs us into thinking? Our thinking keeps to the road and within the domain of traditional thinking. The essential nature of our thinking, however, becomes apparent through the translation of Parmenides' saying. What is determining for the essential nature of λέγειν and νοεῖν, now, is That to which their conjunction conforms. Presumably the two words conform to whatever disposes of λέγειν and νοεῖν, by directing and drawing both to what they both refer to. And that is ἐὸν ἔμμεναι. Ἐὸν ἔμμεναι directs that which constitutes the fundamental character of thinking—the λέγειν and νοεῖν— into its own nature. What so directs is what calls on us to think.

The effort to make an adequate translation of the final words of the saying, the attempt to hear what is expressed in the Greek words ἐὸν ἔμμεναι, is nothing less than the attempt to take to heart That which calls on us to think. To the extent to which we make the effort to take it so to heart, we are asking the question "What is called thinking?" in the decisive fourth sense:

What is That which calls on us to think, by so disposing the conjunction of λέγειν and νοεῖν that it relates to It?

Insofar as we are capable of asking the question in the fourth, decisive sense, we also respond to the third way of asking "What is called thinking?" The third way is intent on arriving at what is needed, and thus required of us, if we are ever to accomplish thinking in an essentially fitting manner. No one knows what is called "thinking" in the sense of the third question until he is capable of λέγειν τε νοεῖν τε.

But as concerns thinking, we are living in the domain of a two-and-one-half-thousand year old tradition. Accordingly, we must not imagine it to be enough for any man merely to inhabit the world of his own representational ideas, and to express only them. For the world of this expression is shot through with blindly adopted and un-re-examined ideas and concepts. How could this confused manner of forming ideas be called thinking, however loudly it may claim to be creative? We are capable of thinking only if we try first of all to develop the question "What is called thinking" in its fourfold sense, and in the light of the decisive fourth question.

A lecture course that ventures on such an undertaking

must set itself limits. This is why we turned the decisive fourth question, "What is That which directs us into thinking?," in the direction of the second, "What is thinking in the traditional sense?"

But this is not an historical inquiry into the various views of thinking which have been formed in the course of its history. Rather, our question is: what is That which directs and disposes us toward the basic characteristics of what in time develops into Western-European thinking? What is it that calls, and to whose call something responds in such a way that it is then called thinking, in the sense of the λέγειν of λόγος, as the νοεῖν of reason? That which calls is what λέγειν and νοεῖν refer to because it relates them to itself, and that means uses them. It is what the saying in its final words calls ἐὸν ἔμμεναι.

We are laboring to translate these words for one reason, and one reason only: our sole question is, what is it that calls on us to think. How else shall we ever hear That which calls, which speaks in thinking, and perhaps speaks in such a way that its own deepest core is left unspoken?

The question of That which calls on us to think gives us the mandate to translate the words ἐὸν ἔμμεναι. But have they not already been translated into the Latin *ens* and *esse*, the English "being" and "to be"? It is indeed superfluous to translate ἐὸν ἔμμεναι into Latin or English. But it is necessary for us to translate these words finally into Greek. Such translation is possible only if we transpose ourselves into what speaks from these words. And this transposition can succeed only by a leap, the leap of a single vision which sees what the words ἐὸν ἔμμεναι, heard with Greek ears, state, or tell.

Can we see something that is told? We can, provided what is told is more than just the sound of words, provided the seeing is more than just the seeing with the eyes of the body. Accordingly, the transposition by the leap of such a vision does not happen of itself. Leap and vision require long, slow preparation, especially if we are to transpose ourselves to *that* word which is not just one word among many.

Ἐόν speaks of what speaks in every word of the language, and not just in every word, but before all else in every conjunction of words, and thus particularly in those junctures of the language which are not specifically put in words. Ἐόν speaks throughout language, and maintains for it the possibility to tell, to state.

We cannot deal here with the preparations needed to make that leap of vision which transposes us into That which speaks from this word. Here we can state directly only what such a leap sees. Whatever has been seen can be demonstrated only by being seen and seen again. What has been seen can never be proved by adducing reasons and counter-reasons. Such a procedure overlooks what is decisive—the looking. If what is seen is put in words, its mention by name can never compel the seeing look. At best, it can offer a token of what a seeing look, renewed again and again, would presumably show more clearly.

Therefore, when we speak of our transposition into ἐόν, and call it that which is seen, such a statement always remains a questioning statement. It looks immediately like a mere assertion, made purely on a whim. That appearance cannot be dispelled directly. Thus it may seem an arbitrary assertion if we now say, in a questioning mode: the word ἐόν indicates what is present, and ἔμμεναι, εἶναι mean "to be present."

What has been gained? We merely replace the accustomed words "being" and "to be" with less accustomed ones—"present" and "to be present." Yet we must admit that the word "to be" always dissipates like a vapor, into every conceivable vague signification, while the word "present" speaks at once more clearly: something present, that is, present to us. Present and presence means: what is with us. And that means: to endure in the encounter.

We may recall here how Kant, at the peak of modern European thinking, in his *Critique of Pure Reason* defines the individual being (ὄν) that is demonstrable in its being. Kant defines being as the object of experience. The object is characterized by enduring in the encounter. The object is characterized by presence, and thus by being here. If the individual being, τὸ ἐόν, were not manifest even as something that is here, beings could never appear as objects. If εἶναι (Being) did not prevail as a being present, the question of the presence of the object, that is, of the object's objectivity, could not even be asked. If the ἐόν ἔμμεναι, in the sense of the being here of what is present, did not prevail, Kant's thinking would have no place in which to make even a single statement of his *Critique of Pure Reason*. Nor is this all.

If the Being of beings, in the sense of the being here of what is present, did not already prevail, beings could not have appeared as objects, as what is objective in objects—and only by such objectivity do they become available to the ideas and propositions in the positing and disposing of nature by which we constantly take inventory of the energies we can wrest from nature. This disposition of nature according to its energy supply arises from the hidden essence of modern technology.

If εἶναι, Being of beings, did not prevail—in the sense of the being here and thus objectivity of the inventory of objects—not only would the airplane engines fail to function, they would not exist. If the Being of beings, as the being here of what is present, were not manifest, the electric energy of the atom could never have made its appearance, could never have put man to work in its own way —work in every respect determined by technology.

It may thus be of some importance whether we hear

what the decisive rubric of Western-European thinking, ἐόν, says—or whether we fail to hear it.

It probably depends on this Either/Or whether or not we will get beyond our talk about technology and finally arrive at a relation to its *essential nature*. For we must first of all respond to the nature of technology, and only afterward ask whether and how man might become its master. And that question may turn out to be nonsensical, because the essence of technology stems from the presence of what is present, that is, from the Being of beings—something of which man never is the master, of which he can at best be the servant.

The first service man can render is to give thought to the Being of beings, and that is first of all to pay it heed. A remote preparation therefor is the attempt to give heed, in questioning, to what the word ἐόν says. The word says: presence of what is present. What it says *speaks* in our speech long before thinking gives attention and a name of its own to it. When thinking is expressed, this unspoken something is merely clothed in a word. It is not an invention but a discovery, discovered in the presence of the present already expressed in language.

Greek thinking, even before its beginnings, is at home with the prevalence of ἐόν as the presence of what is present. Only thus can thinking be awakened and called upon to take to heart the present, in respect of its presence. If that happens—and it does happen in the thinking of the Greek thinkers from Parmenides to Aristotle—it is still no assurance that such thinking will also clothe the presence of what is present, in words, with all possible clarity and in every respect. Even more, it remains undecided whether in the "presence of what is present" there will appear That which constitutes the presence of what is present. It would be a mistake, then, for us to take the view that Being of beings meant merely, for all time, the presence of what is present.

Of course, the essential nature of presence alone gives us enough to think about. And even *this*—what the presence of that which is present might mean in its Greek sense—has not been adequately traced in our inquiry.

Not everything that in some way is, is present in the same way. But we shall now try to bring out at least some of the fundamental characteristics of the presence of what is present. But why do we translate the Greek εἶναι and ἐόν with "being present"? Because in the Greek, εἶναι must always be supplied tacitly and is often made explicit: παρεῖναι and ἀπεῖναι. The πάρά means coming closer; the ἀπό, going away.

The Greeks do not conceive of being present and abiding primarily in terms of mere duration. For the Greeks, a totally different trait predominates in being present and abiding—at times specifically expressed through πάρά and ἀπό. To be present is to come close by, to be here in contrast and conflict with to be away. But whence does the presence come closer—and closer to what?

A mountain range that lies before us may serve as an example. We give our attention to the mountains that are there, not in respect of their geological structure or geographical location, but only in respect of their being present. What is present has risen from unconcealment. It takes its origin from such a rise in its being present. Having risen from unconcealment, what is present also has entered into what was already unconcealed: the mountain range lies in the landscape. Its presence is the rising entry into what is unconcealed within unconcealment, even and especially when the mountain range keeps standing as it is, extending and jutting.

But this rise from unconcealment, as the entry into what is unconcealed, does not specifically come to the fore in the presence of what is present. It is part of presence to hold back these traits, and thus to let come out only that which is present. Even, and in particular, that unconcealment in which this rise and entry takes place, remains concealed, in contrast to the unconcealed present things.

The presence we described gathers itself in the continuance which causes a mountain, a sea, a house to endure and, by that duration, to lie before us among other things that are present. All lying-before-us is already constituted in presence. And presence itself? Presence itself is precisely the presence *of* what is present, and remains so even if we specifically stress its various traits. Presence does demand unconcealment, and is a rising from unconcealment—though not generally but in such a way that presence is the entry into a duration of unconcealment. The Greeks experience such duration as a luminous appearance in the sense of illumined, radiant self-manifestation. Continuance is the coming-to-the-fore that is at rest, has come to rest before the unconcealedness of what lies before us. Rest in duration is not, however, the absence of movement. Rest, in the presence of what is present, is a gathering. It gathers the rising to the coming-to-the-fore, with the hidden suddenness of an ever-possible absenting into concealedness. The παρά in the εἶναι, the coming into present being and being present, does not mean that what is present comes *toward us* men as an object. The παρά means nearness, in the sense of the radiance issuing from unconcealedness into unconcealedness. What has come near in such nearness may be very distant.

Wherever the thinking of the Greeks gives heed to the presence of what is present, the traits of presence which we mentioned find expression: unconcealedness, the rising from unconcealedness, the entry into unconcealedness, the coming and the going away, the duration, the gathering, the radiance, the rest, the hidden suddenness of possible absenting. These are the traits of presence in whose terms the Greeks thought of what is present. But they never *gave thought* to the traits themselves, for presence did *not* become problematical, questionable to them as the presence of *what* is present. Why not? Because the only thing for which *they* asked, and perhaps had to ask, responded and replied, that is, answered to their questioning in these traits of presence which we mentioned.

Subsequent European thinking, by asking the question τί τὸ ὄν, is set on the appointed road. The presence of what is present becomes for it even less problematical. In fact, it more and more loses track of the traits of presence, to favor other traits. The other traits in the Being of beings—the objectivity of the object which we mentioned, the reality of the real—are nonetheless still constituted in the fundamental character of presence; just as in all subjectivity the ὑποκείμενον still shines through, that which is present as what lies before us—and corresponding to it in terms of intellectual grasping and conceiving, is the modified letting-lie-before-us, λέγειν as the λόγος of logic. This rubric, after it was prepared in Kant's "transcendental logic," reaches the highest meaning possible in metaphysics through Hegel. "Logic" here means the ontology of absolute subjectivity. This "logic" is not a discipline, it is part of the matter itself; in the sense of Being, as Being is thought of in Hegel's metaphysics, it is the Being of beings as a whole.

Western logic finally becomes logistics, whose irresistible development has meanwhile brought forth the electronic brain, whereby man's nature and essence is adapted and fitted into the barely noticed Being of beings that appears in the nature of technology.

Do we attend now in a more questioning attitude than before to what the words ἐόν ἔμμεναι designate, the presence of what is present? Perhaps, and if so, then best by renouncing any notion that we could succeed at the first attempt, without long preparation. Public opinion today cherishes the notion that the thinking of thinkers must be capable of being understood in the same way as the daily newspaper. That all men cannot all follow the thought processes of modern theoretical physics is considered quite in order. But to learn the thinking of thinkers is in essence much more difficult, not because this thinking is still more involved but because it is simple—too simple for the easy fluency of common notions.

The ἐὸν ἔμμεναι, according to the saying, is That to which the λέγειν τε νοεῖν τε must remain directed, so that from the conjunction of the two there may develop the nature of thinking which is subsequently decisive. That means: the ἐὸν ἔμμεναί lays claim to the λέγειν τε νοεῖν τε for itself, in respect of itself. Only if the letting-lie-before-us and the taking-to-heart conform and join themselves to the ἐὸν ἔμμεναι, and remain dependent and focused on the ἐὸν ἔμμεναι, will their conjunction be sufficient to the nature of thinking that is required by the ἐὸν ἔμμεναι. The χρή, "it is useful," speaks through the ἐὸν ἔμμεναι, the presence of what is present. The ἐὸν ἔμμεναι, in a veiled fashion, names the "It" in χρή, "It is useful." The ἐὸν ἔμμεναι therefore names that which calls thinking into its essential nature, into the conjunction of λέγειν and νοεῖν. That conjunction determines to what extent subsequent thinking defines itself as διαλέγεσθαι and διανοεῖσθαι. Their nature is henceforth directed by logic and dialectic, logic as dialectic. The name "logic" achieves its highest dignity when it becomes the title of the supreme peak of Western metaphysics. It then designates what, in Hegel's *Phenomenology of Spirit*, the spirit prepares for itself as its own element, in which its moments "extend in the *form of simplicity*" and "organise into the whole." The movement of this organization of the Absolute is the *"Logic or Speculative Philosophy"* (see Preface to *Phenomenology of Spirit*).

In ἐὸν ἔμμεναι is concealed the call that calls into the thinking of the West.

If that is how the matter stands, the situation can be presented in a still more succinct form. We are simply following the manner of presentation which Parmenides himself considers indicated. Instead of λέγειν τε νοεῖν τε, he most often says merely νοεῖν, taking-to-heart. Instead of ἐὸν ἔμμεναι he merely says εἶναι, or else simply ἐόν.

As the situation has been presented, νοεῖν—translated for short as thinking—is thinking only to the extent to which it remains dependent and focused on the εἶναι, Being. Νοεῖν is not "thinking" simply by virtue of occurring as a non-material activity of soul and spirit. Νοεῖν qua νοεῖν belongs together with εἶναι, and thus belongs to εἶναι itself.

Does Parmenides say such a thing? He does indeed, for instance in the saying identified as fragment 5, and again in the large fragment 8, 34 ff.

The first passage runs:

"τὸ γὰρ αὐτὸ νοεῖν ἐστίν τε καὶ εἶναι"

The usual translation is:

"For it is the same thing to think and to be."

However, in translating the saying we discussed before, we have learned to discern more precisely: εἶναι means ἐὸν ἔμμεναι, presence of what is present; while νοεῖν belongs in *one single* conjunction with λέγειν and signifies "taking-to-heart." But what does τὸ αὐτό mean in the passage just cited? It is correctly translated with "the same." What does that mean? Is its meaning identical with "of a kind"? By no means. For, first, τὸ αὐτό never has that meaning, and second—as the saying translated earlier makes clear—Parmenides is far from holding the view that Being and thinking are of a kind, so that we could indifferently substitute thinking for being, and being for thinking. But per-

haps τὸ αὐτό, the same, can be understood in the sense of
"identical." In current speech we constantly interchange
the expressions "identical" and "the same." But "identical"
in Greek is ὅμοιον, not αὐτό. Indeed, how can thinking and
being ever be identical? They are precisely what is different: presence of what is present, and taking-to-heart.

But it is just in their difference that they do belong
together. Where and how? What is the element in which
they belong together? Is it the νοεῖν, or the εἶναι, or neither?
Is it, then, a third thing which in truth is the first for both
—the first not as their synthesis, but still more primary and
more originary than any thesis? We learned: νοεῖν conceived in separation and by itself, that is, conceived without
and apart from any relation to εἶναι, is simply not thinking
at all. If confirmation were needed, Parmenides himself
tells us so emphatically in the other passage, fragment 8,
34 ff.:

"οὐ γὰρ ἄνευ τοῦ ἐόντος . . . εὑρήσεις τὸ νοεῖν"
"for not separately from the presence of what is present
can you find out the taking-to-heart."

When Parmenides here says ἄνευ τοῦ ἐόντος rather than
ἄνευ τοῦ εἶναι, he does so probably for substantive, not just
stylistic reasons. The word ἄνευ means "without" in the
sense of apart from; ἄνευ is the relation opposite to σύν,
together. Ὄν γὰρ ἄνευ—for not apart from . . . but
rather only together with: the γάρ, for, refers to ταὐτόν,
τὸ αὐτό, the same. Accordingly, what does the word τὸ αὐτό,
the same, mean? It means what belongs together.

"τὸ γὰρ αὐτὸ νοεῖν ἐστίν τε καὶ εἶναι"
"for the same: taking-to-heart is so also presence of what
is present."

The two belong together in this way, that the essential
nature of νοεῖν, named first, consists in its remaining fo-

cused on the presence of what is present. Ἐόν, the presence of what is present, accordingly keeps and guards νοεῖν within itself as what belongs to it. From ἐόν, the presence of what is present, there speaks the duality of the two. There speaks from it the call that calls us into the essential nature of thinking, that admits thinking into its own nature and there keeps and guards it.

How is this so? Why and in what way is thinking directed and called into its own essential nature by the Being of beings? *That* it is so, Parmenides states unequivocally in fragments 5 and 8, 34/36. Parmenides, it is true, does not speak of the call. However, he does say: in the presence of what is present there speaks the call that calls us into thinking, the call that calls thinking into its own nature in this way, that it directs νοεῖν into εἶναι.

But in the second of the two passages just cited, Parmenides gives a decisive indication why and how νοεῖν belongs together with εἶναι. To follow this indication through, more is required than this course of lectures could provide. We would first have to give thought to the essential nature of language, in respect of what was said earlier concerning λέγειν and λόγος. It remains obscure why precisely ἐὸν ἔμμεναι calls us into thought, and in what way. Let us note well—ἐὸν ἔμμεναι, the presence of what is present, and not what is present as such and not Being as such, nor both added together in a synthesis, but: their duality, emerging from their unity kept hidden, keeps the call.

Another thing, however, is clear: the saying τὸ γὰρ αὐτὸ νοεῖν ἐστίν τε καὶ εἶναι becomes the basic theme of all of Western-European thinking. The history of that thinking is at bottom a sequence of variations on this one theme, even where Parmenides' saying is not specifically cited. The most magnificent variation, which, despite all the variance of its basic metaphysical position, matches in its greatness the majesty of early Greek thinking, is that proposition of Kant which he thinks as the supreme principle of all *a priori* synthetic judgments. What Kant calls synthetic judgments *a priori* is the modern interpretation of the λέγειν τε νοεῖν τ' ἐὸν ἔμμεναι. In that proposition, Kant tells us that, and how, thinking—the forming of ideas concerning the Being of empirical beings—belongs together with the Being of beings. But for Kant, the individual being appears as an object of experience. "Being" indicates the objectivity of the object.

The variation of Parmenides' statement runs:

"The conditions of the *possibility of experience* in general are at the same time conditions of the *possibility of the objects of experience*" (*Critique of Pure Reason*, A 158, B 197). The "at the same time" is Kant's interpretation of τὸ αὐτό, "the same."

What this statement says is radically different from what Parmenides' saying (fragment 5) says. Parmenides' statement cannot, therefore, be interpreted in Kant's terms, while the reverse is both possible and necessary. Though Kant says something absolutely different, his thinking moves nonetheless in the same (not the identical) sphere as the thinking of the Greek thinkers. What Parmenides says in τὸ γὰρ αὐτὸ νοεῖν ἐστίν τε καὶ εἶναι is different also from the statement by which Hegel transposes and transmutes Kant's principle into the Absolute, when he says that "Being is Thinking" (Preface to *Phenomenology of Spirit*).

Our questioning can arrive at what is called thinking only if we pay heed to what we are called to do—λέγειν τε νοεῖν τ'ἐὸν ἔμμεναι, and with it to be on the quest and lookout for what calls, the ἐὸν ἔμμεναι, the presence of what is present, the duality of what the *one* word, the participle of participles, the word ἐόν designates: what is present in presence.

"What is called thinking?" At the end we return to the question we asked at first when we found out what our word "thinking" originally means. *Thanc* means memory, thinking that recalls, thanks.

But in the meantime we have learned to see that the essential nature of thinking is determined by what there is to be thought about: the presence of what is present, the Being of beings. Thinking is thinking only when it *recalls* in thought the ἐόν, That which this word indicates properly and truly, that is, unspoken, tacitly. And that is the duality of beings and Being. This quality is what properly gives food for thought. And what is so given, is the gift of what is most worthy of question.

Can thinking take this gift into its hands, that is, take it to heart, in order to entrust it in λέγειν, in the telling statement, to the original speech of language?